# Santa Barbara
# Secrets & Sidetrips

*A Guide to the Lesser Known Attractions and the Inns of Santa Barbara and Ventura Counties*
*by*

## Laurie MacMillan

Shoreline Press
SANTA BARBARA • 2002

ISBN 1-885375-03-4

Published by Shoreline Press
Post Office Box 3562
Santa Barbara, California 93130.

Design and typography by Jim Cook

Cover art and illustrations by Alan Freeman, whose work can be seen at Santa Barbara's Sunday Arts and Crafts Show on Cabrillo Boulevard.

Photographs on pages 1 and 22 by John Woodward; photograph on page 78 courtesy of The Wildling Museum; photograph on page 101 courtesy of the Inn of the Spanish Garden; photograph on page 111 courtesy of the Inn on Summer Hill; photograph on page 113 courtesy of the Ballard Inn; all other photographs by Laurie MacMillan.

ACKNOWLEDGMENTS

Special thanks go to Gene and Carol Servin of Incentive Destination Productions, who gave me the job of searching out new attractions for guided tours, thereby starting me on the path that led to this book. My husband, Thad, gave me invaluable help and encouragement along the way, and people involved with all the attractions assisted me cheerfully. In addition, I'd like to thank the following people for giving me information and suggestions:

Mary Gosselin, former Curator of Education,
Santa Barbara Museum of Natural History
Cathleen Grabowski, former Lotusland docent
David Griggs, Curator, Carpinteria Valley Museum of History
Lynne Norris, Los Olivos-based writer
Michael Redmon, Director of Research, Santa Barbara Historical Museum
Richard Senate, Ventura historian
Gene Stevens, Lompoc Chamber of Commerce
Adrian Wilkins, motorcycle enthusiast

# Santa Barbara
# *Secrets & Sidetrips*

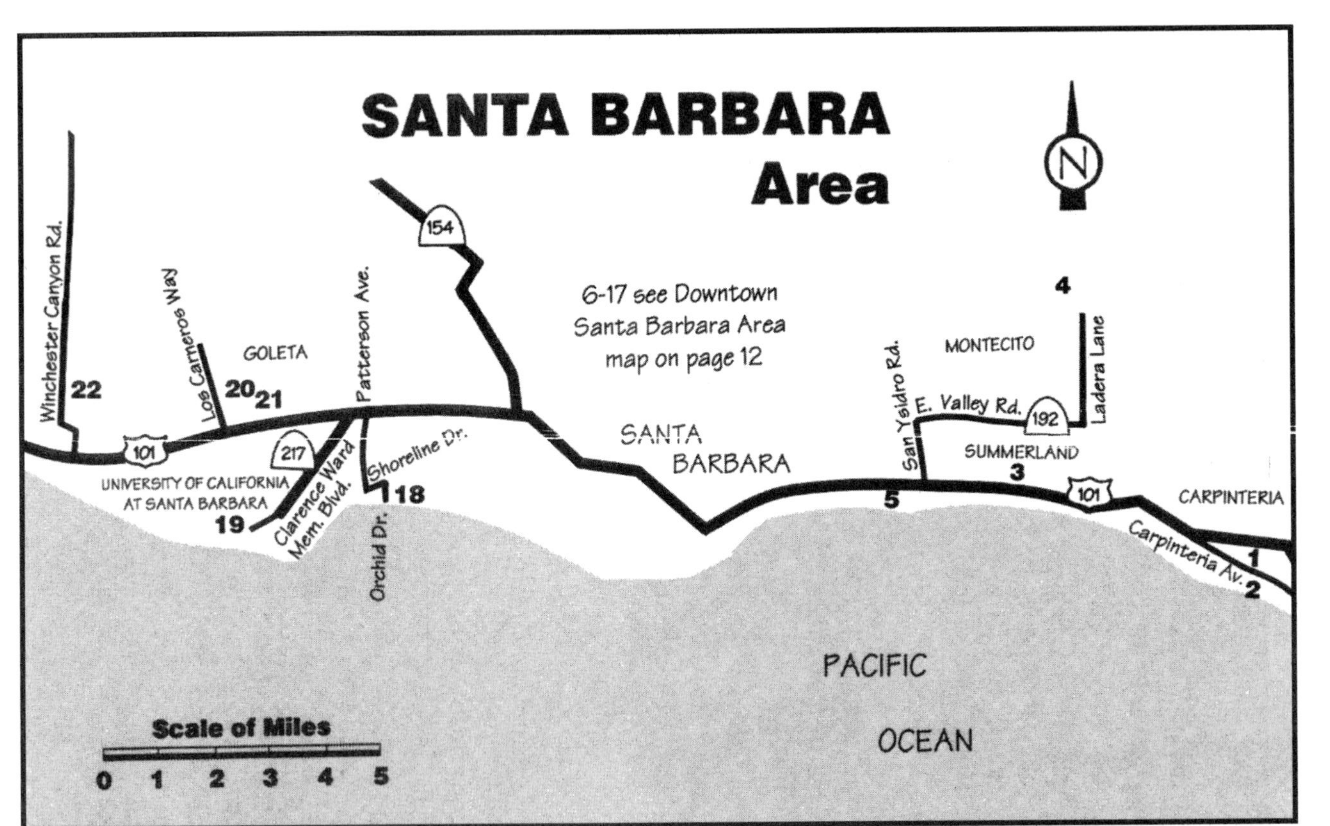
SANTA BARBARA
Area
N
6-17 see Downtown
Santa Barbara Area
map on page 12
Winchester Canyon Rd.
22
Los Carneros Way
GOLETA
20
21
Patterson Ave.
154
101
217
UNIVERSITY OF CALIFORNIA
AT SANTA BARBARA
19
Clarence Ward
Mem. Blvd.
Shoreline Dr.
18
Orchid Dr.
SANTA
BARBARA
San Ysidro Rd.
E. Valley Rd.
192
MONTECITO
4
Ladera Lane
SUMMERLAND
3
5
101
CARPINTERIA
Carpinteria Av.
1
2
PACIFIC
OCEAN
Scale of Miles
0
1
2
3
4
5

# Table of Contents

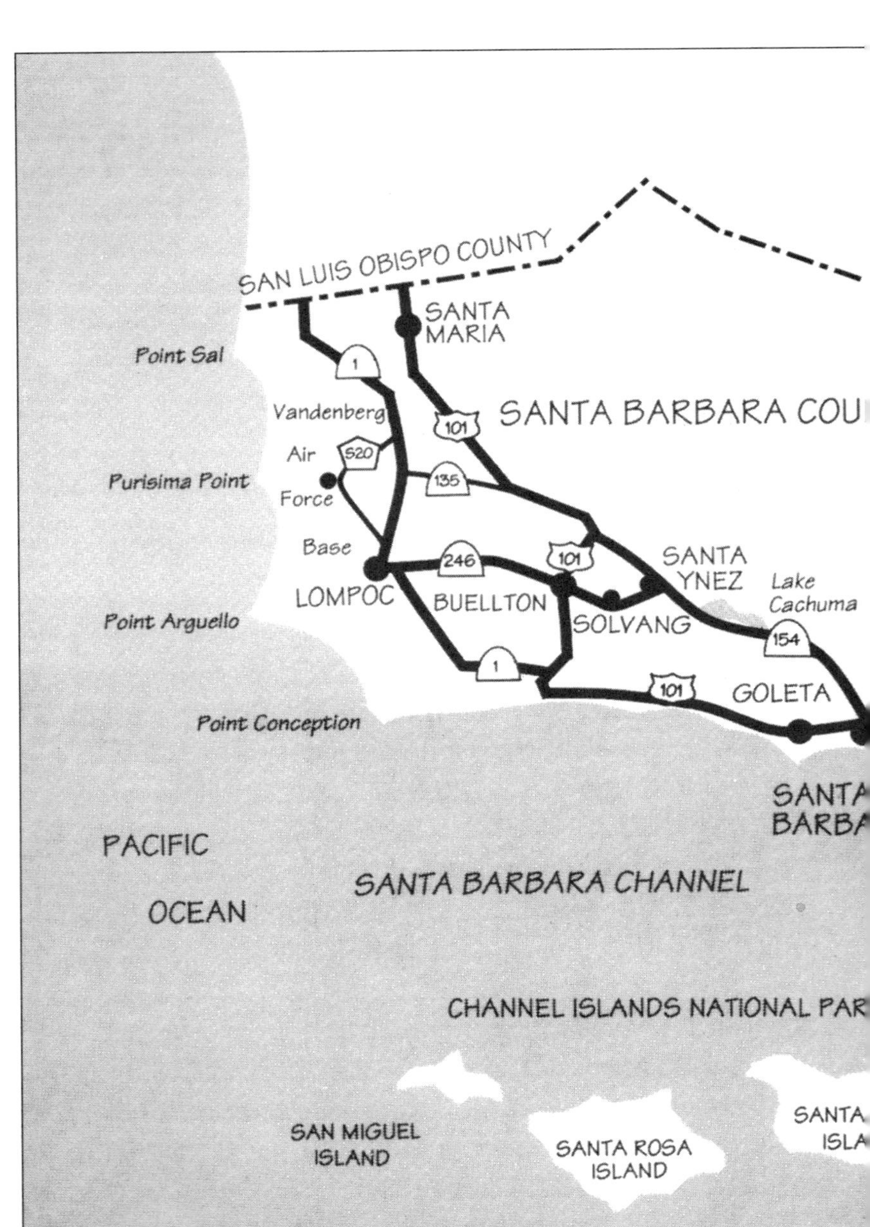
SAN LUIS OBISPO COUNTY
SANTA MARIA
Point Sal
1
Vandenberg Air Force Base
101
520
Purisima Point
135
246
101
SANTA YNEZ
Lake Cachuma
LOMPOC
BUELLTON
SOLVANG
Point Arguello
154
1
101
GOLETA
Point Conception
PACIFIC OCEAN
SANTA BARBARA CHANNEL
SAN MIGUEL ISLAND
SANTA ROSA ISLAND

# SANTA BARBARA and Ventura Counties

# How to Use This Book

YOU say that you've already seen Santa Barbara's mission and Stearns Wharf? Once you've seen Santa Barbara's major attractions, how about visiting the places that AAA never mentioned? Even if you've taken the trolley around town and made an excursion to some of the well-known wineries, there's more. Have you seen the photographic college in the hills overlooking Santa Barbara or the seal sanctuary in Carpinteria? How about making a trip to a scenic ranch where you can pick your own oranges, or taking a paragliding lesson?

This book will be of greatest help to people who already have some familiarity with Santa Barbara and northern Ventura counties. You may live here, or perhaps you've visited before, have enjoyed what the area has to offer, and want to see more. While this is not meant to be a comprehensive guidebook, the new visitor will find a section that briefly lists the major attractions of Santa Barbara. No attempt has been made to catalog restaurants and motels, but we did highlight the area's fine bed-and-breakfast inns. In other words, you're holding a selection of lesser-known yet fun, scenic, interesting, or informative places to go when you have some free time to explore. Reading the City Sketch before you visit a town may heighten your appreciation for its individual character. You'll particularly enjoy your forays if you strike up conversations with the locals about what they do and the area in which they live. People usually love to talk about themselves, and we hope you'll give them the opportunity to do just that. You'll learn something if you do.

This book is arranged by type of attraction, and there is a

geographical index in the back. So if you wish to see which listings are in a particular town, regardless of the kind of attraction, see page 119. Most places are free to visit. If not, it will be indicated, and bed-and-breakfast price ranges are shown from the lowest weekday rate, to the highest weekend rate, unless noted otherwise. All of the phone listings are in the 805 area code, so area codes have been omitted in the text information.

Undoubtedly you will know of some of the places listed. Our goal is to excite you about the ones you haven't seen, so that you'll go out and and explore, even if you've lived in the area for a long time. Always take with you a detailed map, and remember that most of the places listed here are small operations and things change. Whenever possible, reconfirm the hours open or other pertinent details before you set out, and make a reservation where indicated. Be flexible, be curious, and have fun!

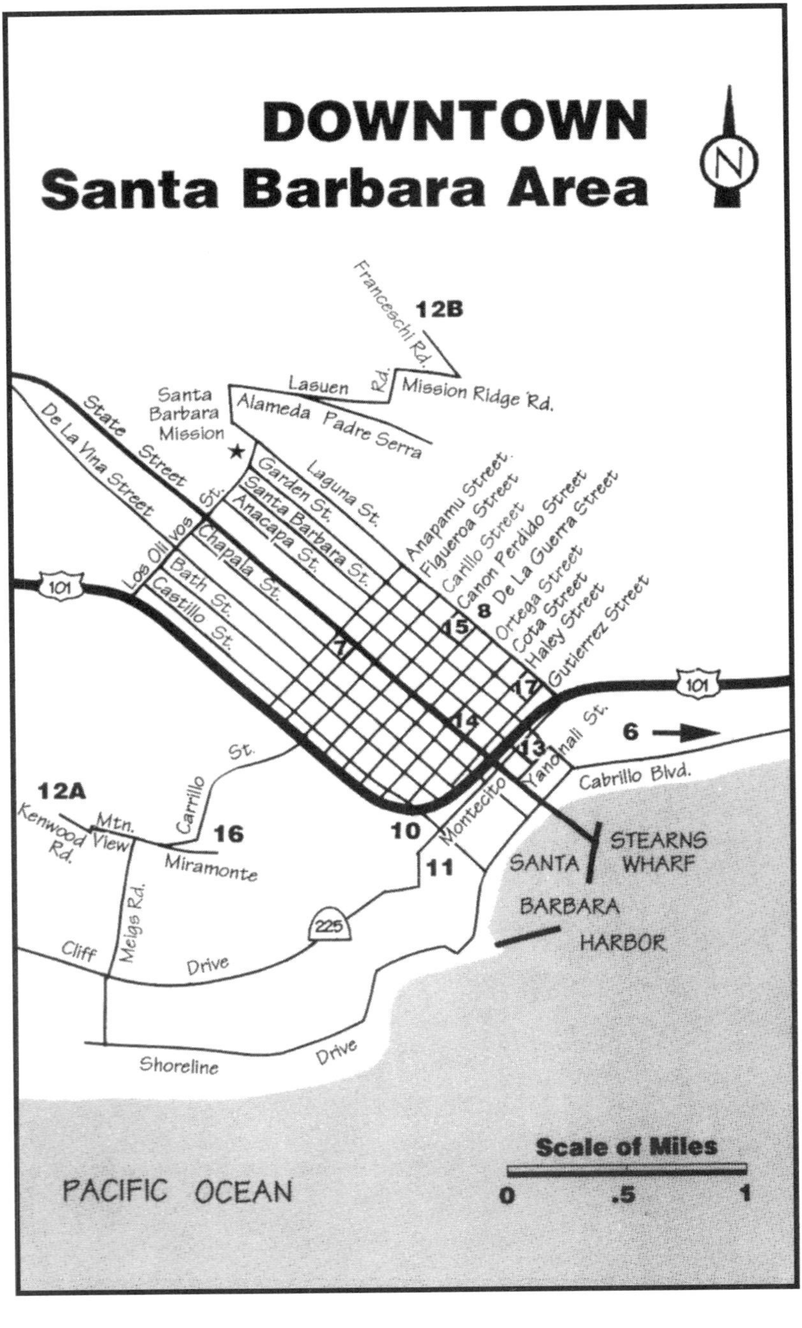

# DOWNTOWN
# Santa Barbara Area

12B
Franceschi Rd.
Rd.
Lasuen
Mission Ridge Rd.
Santa Barbara Mission
Alameda Padre Serra
State Street
De La Vina Street
Garden St.
Laguna St.
Santa Barbara St.
Anacapa St.
Los Olivos St.
Chapala St.
Bath St.
Castillo St.
101
Anapamu Street
Figueroa Street
Carillo Street
Canon Perdido Street
De La Guerra Street
Ortega Street
Cota Street
Haley Street
Gutierrez Street
8
15
7
17
101
14
13
Yanonali St.
6
Cabrillo Blvd.
St.
Carrillo
12A
Kenwood Rd.
Mtn. View
16
Miramonte
10
Montecito
11
STEARNS WHARF
SANTA BARBARA HARBOR
225
Meigs Rd.
Cliff Drive
Shoreline Drive
PACIFIC OCEAN
Scale of Miles
0 .5 1

# Santa Barbara's Major Attractions

ALTHOUGH this book is focusing on the attractions of the area that may not be immediately obvious to visitors, you should also make a point of seeing the most significant spots. So here are some facts about Santa Barbara's main enticements. We suggest that you obtain a free map from the Visitor Center at the corner of Santa Barbara Street and Cabrillo Boulevard, which indicates the locations.

**Botanic Garden, 1212 Mission Canyon Road, 682-4726.** Sixty spectacular acres of native plants in a mountain setting. Open daily, winter 9 to 4 weekdays, 9 to 5 weekends. Spring through fall 9 to 5 weekdays, 9 to 6 weekends. $5 for adults, call for tour times.

*The Santa Barbara County Courthouse has often been called one of America's most beautiful public buildings.*

**Casa de la Guerra, 11-25 E. De la Guerra St., 966-9719.** 1827 Presidio Comandante's home, now operated by the Trust for Historic Preservation. Rotating historical displays. Open Thursday through Sunday, 12 to 4, donation.

**County Courthouse, 1100 Anacapa Street, 962-6464.** Spanish-Moorish "castle" with panoramic view from clock tower. Open weekdays 8:30 to 4:30, weekends and holidays 10 to 4:30. No admission charge, donations welcome. Free tours, call for times.

**El Paseo, 15 East De La Guerra Street.** Historic Spanish-style courtyard with two charming restaurants.

**El Presidio de Santa Barbara (State Historic Park), 122 East Canon Perdido Street, 966-9719.** Ongoing reconstruction of one of the four Spanish forts founded in California in the 1700s. Site of extensive archaeology. Visitor Center contains fort model, photos and pictures, displays. Slide show available for viewing, and books for sale. Open daily 10:30 to 4:30, donations welcome.

**Historical Museum, 136 East De La Guerra Street, 966-1601.** Displays of art and artifacts from Santa Barbara's Spanish, Mexican, and American periods. Beautiful Spanish-style courtyard, adjacent to Covarrúbias and Historic Adobes. Open 10 to 5. Tuesday through Saturday, noon to 5 on Sunday. Call for tour times. Donations appreciated.

**Lotusland, Montecito, 969-9990.** Fabulous 25-acre fantasy garden created by the late Madame Ganna Walska. Docent-led tours through the shade, theater, Japanese, aloe, blue, and lotus gardens. See the largest cycad collection in America, which Madame Walska financed by selling her diamond and emerald jewelry. Reservations mandatory, sometimes up to one year ahead. Admission charge.

**Maritime Museum, Breakwater, 962-8404.** Interactive displays showing area's maritime history, commercial fishing and diving,

*Founded in 1786, Mission Santa Barbara is known as the "Queen of the Missions."*

yachting, shipwrecks and more. Summer open 11-6, closed Wednesday. Nov.-June open 11-5, closed Tuesday and Wednesday. Adults $5.

**Mission Santa Barbara, 2201 Laguna Street, 682-4713.** Self-guided tour of museum, mission-life displays, church, and cemetery. Open daily 9 to 5, $4 for adults, children under 11 free.

**Museum of Art, 1130 State Street, 963-4364.** Outstanding permanent collection and special exhibits. Open Tuesday-Saturday 11 to 5 (Friday til 9), Sunday 12 to 5. $6 adults, $4 seniors, $2 students and kids over 5. Free on Thursdays.

**Museum of Natural History, 2559 Puesta Del Sol Road, 682-4711.** Open daily 10 to 5. Admission $7, seniors and teens $6, children $4.

**Santa Barbara Arts and Crafts Show, on Cabrillo Boulevard east of State Street, 962-8956.** America's longest-running weekly outdoor fine-art and crafts show. All items are designed, handcrafted, and sold by artists residing in Santa Barbara County. Every Sunday from 10 a.m. to dusk.

**Stearns Wharf & Santa Barbara Harbor.** West Coast's oldest operating wooden wharf and scenic yacht harbor. Both have shops, restaurants, and boat tours. Sailboat and jet boat rentals at harbor (see Sports City, page 90).

**Zoological Gardens, 500 Ninos Drive (off Cabrillo Boulevard), 962-5339.** Named a model for small zoos in America. Open 10 to 5 daily. $8 for adults, $6 seniors and children 2-12.

After you've visited any places above that interest you, you're ready to start enjoying Santa Barbara's "secrets," and maybe do a little sidetripping.

*The Santa Barbara Zoo is a fun place for kids of all ages.*

# City Sketches

YOU may not be a history buff. If you are, the thumbnail historical sketches that follow may seem too brief. But they're meant to be a starting point and should provide enough information to help the casual visitor appreciate the character of each town. After all, if you aren't aware of the influences that came to bear on a place, how can you know what you're looking at?

## ◆ *The Cultivation of Carpinteria*

When the Spaniards first arrived, beautiful oaks with hanging moss covered large parts of the Carpinteria Valley. There were natural tar seepages near the beach, which were used by Chumash Indians to caulk their canoes (called *tomols*) and waterproof their baskets. This same tar would become handy at the Presidio for roofing and flooring material. Because of the Indian boat carpenters, the area was given its name, which is Spanish for "the carpenter shop." The land came under the control of the Santa Barbara pueblo. Local Indians were hired to clear the oaks, ushering in the great and still-present era of agriculture in the Carpinteria Valley.

Through trial and error, farmers found those agricultural products that were most profitable. When American settlers came in, they bought up land in Carpinteria, or married into the local Mexican families, and grew nuts, vegetables, and lemons. Carpinteria holds the (perhaps dubious) honor of being the first place in the U.S. to grow lima beans commercially, and the old packing house still stands near the ocean. But in the nineteenth century, travel and the transporting of crops was tough. Casitas Pass was rugged, and the stagecoach route to Ventura along the coast was slow and had to be timed with the tides.

In 1875 a "boom" started in Carpinteria. A San Francisco firm that dealt in refined tar opened up the tar pits east of Carpinteria Creek. Other companies followed. At the industry's peak, hundreds of men were employed. There was a hotel and cafe near the pits, and six saloons opened on Linden Avenue. It was said that the men really needed a stiff drink after work because the pits were infested with rattlesnakes!

The Carpinteria tar pits closed when the firms found they could more profitably produce tar that results from refining petroleum. Workers moved away, and the saloons closed. The pits became the town dump. Later, the Santa Barbara Museum of Natural History identified evidence of twenty-five species of plants in the pits, along with fifty-five bird fossils and remains of wolf, elephant, ground sloth, and bison.

When the railroad came to Carpinteria in 1887, its scheduled arrivals provided entertainment for the locals, but more important, shipping of the area's produce became much easier. Chinese labor helped build the railroad, and even in 1910 there was still a small Carpinteria Chinatown. About that same time the landmark Palms Hotel was built by a Texan named Isenberg.

Telescoping forward to today, tar seepages can still be seen on the shore, just west of the Seal Sanctuary (see page 64), and there's an oil company pier nearby that services the offshore oil rigs. The Palms Restaurant in the old hotel building is a cook-your-own steak place, and rumor has it that the owner switched to that format after she "fired her last drunk cook." True or not, The Palms dishes up real nostalgia for old timers, along with the other historic restaurant in town, Clementine's.

Farmers have continued to experiment with the wonderful Carpinteria climate. Flower and ground-cover nurseries dominate many acres of surrounding ground, along with avocado orchards, and Carpinteria now hosts the annual Avocado Festival, which draws thousands every October. Several software companies have located there, while many locals struggle to keep more agricultural land from being commercialized. Carpinteria State Beach is touted as "The World's Safest Beach," and one of the most important U.S. venues for the international polo circuit is just outside Carpinteria (call 684-8667 for game information). Many citizens are actively working to preserve Carpinteria's small-town atmosphere and its open spaces, so chances are good that it will be slow to change.

## ◆ *Lompoc: A Little of Everything*

The Chumash Indians used the words *lum poc* to denote a little lake, so when the Spaniards came in 1787 to found a mission, they called the Lompoc area Lumpoco, after the lagoon that used to be there. Later, the mission was moved to its present location at La Purísima Road, but the town wasn't established until 1874. Then businessmen from San Francisco, Santa Barbara, and Santa Cruz formed the Lompoc Valley Land Company to start a temperance colony. They purchased over 40,000 acres of ranch land and subdivided it. Within a month of the land sale, a dozen houses were already built, but this promising start was a false one.

The drought of 1877 led some of the temperance settlers to move away, and those who weren't quite so temperate pushed for their freedom to imbibe. Sheep shearers, who came to Lompoc in spring, liked their liquor, and some of the locals did, too. There were several violent incidents of "gunpowder temperance," including destruction of a drug store where alcohol was sold under the counter. In the end, Lompoc lost its dry status, and settled into an agricultural way of life. They even tried to alter the climate by planting rows of blue gum and cypress trees, which they hoped would raise the temperature for heat-loving lima and pink beans.

Ninety percent of all the mustard seed in the U.S. was grown near Lompoc until the 1940s, when Montana was discovered as a superior spot for that crop. Today Lompoc is considered the flower seed capital of the world (see page 46), and the area also raises vegetables, fruit, nuts, and livestock. Aerospace activity is high, with Vandenberg Air Force Base a big presence; tourism is important, too. Although the town has a few very interesting and historic buildings, most of it is rather prosaic in appearance. But its main attractions for visitors—the flower fields, La Purísima Mission, and the Murals Project (see page 73)—make Lompoc worth a visit.

### ◆ *Los Olivos: It Might Look Like Mayberry, But Look Again*

In 1887 the narrow-gauge Pacific Coast Railway came to Los Olivos. This was the line's southern terminus, and passengers who wanted to travel further south had to continue by stagecoach. Felix Mattei's hostelry in Los Olivos was a busy place, and many expected that the town would see a land boom, but the boom went bust without ever happening. Two land sales were rained out. The stagecoach stopped running when the coastal railroad bypassed Los Olivos in 1901. Then the Pacific Coast Railway from the north stopped its Los Olivos run in 1934, and the town slumbered away for decades.

Finally, in 1976, Cody Gallery opened its doors, and other galleries followed. Sophisticated folks moved to Los Olivos to escape big-city pressures and problems and often to pursue their interest in winemaking, art, or equestrian activities. By 1996 *Worth Magazine*'s list of the 300 U.S. towns with the highest household incomes ranked Los Olivos as number 114, but the town retains its innocent small-town appearance. There's still a flagpole in the middle of the main intersection. Andy Griffith's *Return to Mayberry* was filmed near this pole, where the locals lower the flag to half mast whenever someone from town passes away.

Felix Mattei's place is still in operation as Mattei's Tavern, where you can get a peek at Old West ambience. For a "grander" meal, you might try Fess Parker's Wine Country Inn, where the dining room offers inventive, well-presented food, or for a sandwich, there are a couple of casual, good alternatives.

**Hours:** Brothers Restaurant at Mattei's Tavern (688-4820) offers dinner daily. At the Wine Country Inn (688-7788), all three meals are served seven days.

*The view from Meditation Mount is awe-inspiring.*

## ◆ *Ojai: A "Nest" of Creativity*

The Ojai Valley is a lovely land of gnarled oaks, lush lemon groves, stands of avocado trees, and exotic cherimoyas. Although sometimes prone to smog because of its geography, the views are legendary and its winding country roads a delight. The sight from Dennison Grade is so extraordinary that it was portrayed as Shangri-La in the old movie *Lost Horizons,* starring Ronald Coleman. This is a good spot to wait for Ojai's "pink moment" near sunset, when the Topa Topa Mountains display an other-worldly pink hue. Another place to admire the valley is from Meditation Mount, which is reached via Reeves Road off of Ojai Avenue. Go all the way to the end, follow the signs to the mount, and take the short walk past the meditation building to the overlook point.

The Chumash Indians gave Ojai its name, which means "nest." This refers to the shape given the valley by the surrounding mountains, and perhaps the Chumash also felt that this was a special, protected place. They had a relatively easy existence, living on seeds and nuts, game and seafood. As happened elsewhere in California, their way of life was forever disrupted when the Spaniards came in the 1700s to solidify their hold of the West Coast and to spread Christianity.

ter, when California became a Mexican territory, the government couldn't afford to pay all its soldiers, so it made land grants instead. The entire Ojai Valley was granted to Don Fernando Tico in 1833, and there's still a street named after him. But he eventually sold his land to Americanos, and a town was founded in 1874. It was named Nordhoff after one Charles Nordhoff, whose writings about the West spurred many settlers to head toward California.

The German sound of the name Nordhoff didn't sit well with the townspeople during World War I, so in 1917 they reverted to the Indian name Ojai. That was the year that the wealthy glassware manufacturer, E.D. Libbey, arrived in Ojai from Ohio. He built the Arcade, which is now the focal point for shopping downtown. He also established the Oaks Hotel (which is now a health spa), a Catholic chapel, and the Ojai Valley Inn. The park downtown, which hosts the oldest tennis tournament in the U.S. every April and a music festival in late May-early June, is named after Mr. Libbey.

Ojai has the advantage of being a seemingly isolated, inspiringly beautiful country environment, yet it's within easy distance of Los Angeles. The area has attracted numerous artists, along with philosophical and religious groups, several private schools, and a few accomplished restaurateurs.

There is a spectacular public golf course (Soule Park) with reasonable green fees and a divided bicycle/equestrian trail following the historic Southern Pacific Railroad route. Hiking-trail information can be obtained from the local U.S. Forest Service office at 1190 E. Ojai Avenue, which is open Monday through Saturday. Public tennis courts are in Libbey Park downtown. You can take advantage of all these facilities anytime or attend one of the many special events that Ojai holds throughout the year.

## ◆ *Santa Barbara Overview*

Santa Barbara is a true product of its past and a good example of what happens when you mix wealth and romanticism with a turbulent political and cultural history.

The Spaniards were the first Europeans to arrive here, finding the indigenous Chumash Indians, whose way of life they soon disrupted. The Spanish were afraid that if they didn't protect their ownership of Alta (Upper) California, the Russian fur traders or the English might grab it. So they set out to establish forts, or *presidios,* and one of the four was in Santa Barbara.

The Franciscan priests went along to spread Christianity through the establishment of missions. Padre Junípero Serra would have liked to build Santa Barbara's mission in Montecito, but Padre Fermín Lasuén thought that Montecito was too full of Indians and grizzly bears! To put this all in historic perspective, this mission wasn't founded until 1786, well after the American Revolution.

A quiet military life revolved around the presidio, with an occasional fiesta or traveler being the only entertainment. In 1821 the Mexican Revolution changed Santa Barbara from Spanish to Mexican rule. As the years went on, the Mexican government was unable to pay many of its soldiers. They were given land grants instead, and they proceeded to raise cattle.

Imagine what confronted the first American soldiers to come into Santa Barbara in 1846. The town was foreign territory, with rough adobe architecture, Catholicism, and Spanish language and customs. At that time, and even well after the U.S. planted its flag here, the most powerful men were the Spanish-speaking rancheros. They grew even richer and more influential during the gold rush days. No, they didn't run off to the goldfields. They sold their cattle for exorbitant prices to hungry miners.

In the 1860s, Santa Barbara experienced a terrible drought and almost all of the cattle died. This marked the closing of the Mexican era, which had ended officially years before, and finally in 1870 Santa Barbara's town records started being kept in English.

During the 1870s Santa Barbara began to look like a typical Western town, with wooden sidewalks and false-fronted buildings. It wasn't long before the town became known as a health resort, where wealthy Americans would come for the season to improve themselves with the wonderful climate and sea breezes.

Around the turn of the century a luxury hotel was built, and business moguls including the Rockefellers, Carnegies, and Duponts rolled in on their private luxury railcars. Some of these titans looked around, liked what they saw, and built huge estates in nearby Montecito, where large, wooded properties were available. There they lived wildly opulent lives, while also giving generously to the community. The Museum of Art, the Natural History Museum, the wonderful medical facilities, many parks, the harbor, the Botanic Gardens and other resources all exist in Santa Barbara because of their largesse.

These benefactors cared not only for Santa Barbara's institutions, but also for its appearance. They had already formed a community Plans and Plantings committee before the drastic earthquake of 1925 hit. A good part of Santa Barbara was levelled, but many saw it as opportunity, not disaster. Now they could rebuild the town to reflect its Spanish heritage. What ensued wasn't exactly faithful to Santa Barbara's early appearance. Rather, it became an idealized, red-tile-roofed model of its former self.

Today Montecito is known by some as "Hollywood North." Celebrities and corporate giants have taken over the grand old estates. Unlike the former owners, the majority of the current celebrity residents stick to themselves, participating little in community affairs, but some, like comedian Jonathan Winters, do become involved Santa Barbarans.

It's true that there are a lot of wealthy people in the area. You'll probably notice some effects of this. For instance, there are more banks, brokerage houses, and restaurants per capita than in almost any other town. But that's only part of the story. The area from Goleta to Carpinteria is home to a multiplicity of economic classes and ethnic groups, all contributing to a very rich and vibrant community.

One final note: It's difficult to give directions in Santa Barbara, because the coastline runs east-west, not north-south as you would expect. The directions given in this book for Santa Barbara locations as east or west are relying on the street designations, such as East Haley or West Carrillo streets. This does not necessarily mean that you'll actually be going east or west. Along the ocean, I've pointed you to what you will think is north or south, although you will probably be going east or west. Don't worry, even most locals are disoriented around this one.

## ◆ *Santa Paula: The Citrus Center*

Santa Paula is one of those places that most people pass while driving between 101 and Interstate 5 and never bother to see. But the "Citrus Capital of the World" has its charms, due to the fact that its residents cherish and preserve its past. The downtown is quaint, and the townspeople seem to retain old-fashioned values and small-town friendliness.

The original Spanish land grant, which included the town, was subdivided into small farms by the 1860s, with the county's first commercial orange groves being planted in 1872. In 1880 oil was discovered, leading to the birth of Union Oil. This oil boom attracted more people to Santa Paula, and the well-to-do ones built beautiful Victorian and Craftsman homes. Even today, though, Santa Paula's main business is agriculture, and it's a major distribution point for citrus fruits.

Most people don't think of Santa Paula as a tourist destination, but for those who like history it's worth a visit. There is a charming playhouse with frequent productions, the Santa Paula Theater Center, 525-3073. The best time to visit is the first weekend of the month, when the Santa Paula Airport has its open house, showcasing antique and exotic aircraft (see page 33), and its Aviation Museum is open. Take a stroll through the quaint downtown, which was used as a location for the *Leave It To Beaver* movie. Go by the Union Oil Museum (see page 34), the historic depot with its visitor center, The Mill, and through the town's lovely tree-lined neighborhoods.

## ◆ *Santa Ynez: The Old and New West*

A visitor to the small town of Santa Ynez sees a mixture of historic Western buildings and newer structures designed in a Western motif. It could almost be a modern theme town, but it really did begin in the 1880s as a farm town, surrounded by wheat growers and ranchers raising horses, cattle, and sheep. Locals did business here with a barber, a harness shop, two blacksmiths, and several stores. There was even a millinery store.

In 1888, speculators became convinced that the Southern Pacific Railroad would be built through the Santa Ynez Valley, and they built the grand College Hotel. A two-story Victorian hotel with thirty rooms and a tower, it had a dining room and saloon and even hosted dramatic productions. Stagecoach passengers routinely stayed there, but the railroad never came. In 1901 the stagecoach ceased operations after the rail lines were connected using the coast route, and that was the end of the College Hotel's heyday. In 1935 it burned down, ending Santa Ynez's dream of glory. Meanwhile, much of the valley's business had moved to Solvang after the Danish community was founded, and Santa Ynez remained a backroads village.

Until, that is, the Chumash Indian Reservation decided to operate a casino. After a few false starts, the Chumash Casino at the edge of Santa Ynez now brings thousands of visitors to the area, and there is a new upscale B&B, the Santa Ynez Inn, 1-800-643-5774. Escaping big-city dwellers, including a number of entertainment figures, are attracted to the valley's slow way of life, and tourists coming to Solvang also enjoy seeing the other valley towns.

*Shops in Santa Ynez cater to ranchers and equestrians.*

### ◆ *Solvang: A Day in Denmark à la Disneyland*

Most people who have visited Solvang either like it a lot or hate the place. This is a town of gift shops, bakeries, fudge shops, restaurants, an outlet center, and other tourist attractions. It looks as if it all could have been created by an amusement park developer, which is why some people are put off. What they don't realize is that the inhabitants of the area really are of Danish descent.

The name Solvang appropriately means "sunny fields." It was established in 1911 by Danes from the Midwest, led by a group of Lutheran pastors. They founded Atterdåg College, a Danish folk school (no longer in existence) and in other ways actively recruited more Danish settlers. Their architecture at first was typically Western with some Mexican influences, like other towns nearby. Finally in the 1940s, the townspeople started to make their town reflect their heritage. One story has it that a *Saturday Evening Post* writer visited, became enamored of the Danish community's customs and setting, and wrote about it. However it really happened, outsiders started visiting, and the residents realized that bringing in tourists had some obvious benefits. Voilà, the Danish look was born in California. With careful observation, you can see some of the old Solvang. The arches on the building on Copenhagen Drive near Alisal Road are left over from the Mexican influence earlier in the century.

Solvang's many gift shops and outlets are engrossing if you're a shopper. But if part of your family is bored with it, they can rent bicycles or surreys at 475 First Street, Suite 8, which is accessed most easily from the alley on the back side of Solvang Park. Bicycling is an excellent way to see the beautiful golden mountains, the well-kept ranches, and the green, lush vineyards in the valley. For those not looking for exercise, there is the Elverhoy Museum in a lovely home that was built to resemble the large farmhouses of eighteenth-century Denmark. The Museum houses an art gallery and rooms displaying life in the old country. If you're more interested in Spanish local history, go see the nearby Santa Ynez Mission instead, or try Solvang's Vintage Motorcycle Museum.

When you get hungry, many restaurants serve Danish specialties, which are interesting but not haute cuisine. Try aebleskivers, the round Danish pancakes, for a snack. Alternatively, for good food and a quick escape from Denmark, eat where the locals do, the River Grill at Alisal's River (golf) Course. The River Grill is an attractive, casual dining room with patio seating as well, overlooking the course and the mountains. Eating there feels like joining a country club for a day.

Solvang has numerous motels in several price categories. The Solvang Conference and Visitors Bureau at 688-6144 can help you with lodging information, should you wish to make Solvang your base for a visit to the Santa Ynez Valley.

• **Elverhoy Museum:** 1 to 4 p.m., Wednesday through Sunday, 686-1211. From Copenhagen Drive, turn down Second Street (it only goes one way) and go to Elverhoy Way. Turn right and you'll see the museum on the left at 1624 Elverhoy.

• **Vintage Motorcycle Museum:** 11 a.m. to 5 p.m. Saturday and Sunday, 7 days in summer, 686-9722, 320 Alisal Road, $5 admission.

• **River Grill:** 7:30 a.m. to 5 p.m. Sunday and Monday, 7:30 a.m. to 8 p.m. Tuesday through Thursday, until 9 p.m. Friday and Saturday, 150 Alisal Road. From Highway 246, turn left on Alisal Road. Go past the outlet mall and down the hill. You'll see a golf course with a water hazard ahead on the left. Turn left at the "River Course - The Alisal" sign, and park near the modern building at the end of the drive which houses the restaurant and pro shop.

## ◆ *Metamorphosis: Spooksville to Summerland*

In recent years Summerland has become known for its antique stores, and the tiny beach town is also home to two distinguished institutions, the Bikini Factory and that great hamburger joint, the Nugget, which has been patronized by President and Mrs. Clinton. The town used to be populated mostly by surfer types who lived in little bungalows. Now a different group has come in, building expensive homes and leading a lifestyle that doesn't revolve around the beach. Shifting tides in this town are nothing new, however.

This little area perched on a hill overlooking the sea was first developed by a spiritualist named Williams in the 1880s. He attracted followers by offering small, cheap lots for sale. Santa Barbarans called the spot "Spooksville" because they were wary of the séances, mediums, and reported ghosts. Williams actually named it Summerland because that was the name of one of the spiritualists' seven heavens.

The next wave to hit Summerland took care of all this spookiness. Oil was discovered, and soon offshore rigs were thick along the coast. Mr. Williams fell into an oil well himself, dying soon thereafter. According to one legend, his widow moved into what is now the Big Yellow House restaurant, and there are still earthbound spirits there.

When the oil supply played out, the rigs were removed, and Summerland fell into the sleepy state it stayed in for years. Now it's woken up, perhaps because of current demand for ocean-view properties. Fortunately, Summerland's hilly and sometimes unstable topography, together with the county building regulations, should keep it from getting too huge. Today it's worth stopping there to browse the antique stores.

## ◆ *A View of Ventura*

Ventura, like Santa Barbara, is a mission town, but this mission was all-powerful because there was no presidio. In the 1830s, however, the missions were secularized, so they no longer controlled huge tracts of land, and in 1846 the mission was sold to a rancher. The Mexican government made land grants to lucky applicants, and nineteen ranchos emerged in Ventura County. After California became U.S. territory during the gold rush, the rancheros were prosperous, but their days were numbered. Farmers and fruit growers began buying up available land, but they weren't the only ones interested in Ventura property. Some of the ranchos were bought by eastern capitalists, who had received favorable reports of petroleum deposits in the area.

Population growth remained slow because Ventura was isolated. Even when the first coast stageline began operation from Santa Barbara in 1868, travel was still unsure. Passengers were often held up by high tides, or worse, by bandits. A wharf was built in Ventura in 1872, making steamer travel easier and access to Ventura more practical. The 1870s saw the first land boom in the city, which went through an architectural metamorphosis from adobes and false-fronted wooden buildings to two-story brick structures.

Another transportation landmark occurred in 1887 when the coast line of the Southern Pacific Railroad came to town. Then there was a second land boom. Hotels were opened, streets were graded, and sidewalks put in. Formerly named San Buenaventura, the town's name was shortened by the railroad, because the whole name wouldn't fit on their timetable!

By the 1920s, oil discoveries were the big news of the day. Two big gushers in the Ventura Avenue field fueled the "Roaring '20s," when Ventura's population grew 179 percent to a whopping 11,603 by 1930. Today oil and agriculture are still the biggest income producers for the county, and the city's large employers include hotels, health care facilities, and government agencies. Tourism has been furthered by the construction of the Ventura Marina, the restoration of historic structures, and the recent refurbishment of downtown Ventura. The art scene is expanding because artists who are refugees from Los Angeles find it to be more peaceful and artists from Santa Barbara like its lower cost of housing.

Unlike Santa Barbara, Ventura never attracted the numbers of wildly wealthy and philanthropic people who gave Santa Barbara so many of its cultural and recreational resources. So Ventura's charms are perhaps a little "funkier," but it's still worth getting to know.

# Highlights from History

**Carriage Museum, 129 Castillo Street, Santa Barbara, 962-2353.** Santa Barbara has a traditional five-day Fiesta every August, with activities ranging from colorful parades to carnivals, street dances, Mexican dance shows and music concerts, and lots of private parties. The group that is responsible for putting on this celebration, Old Spanish Days, collected carriages that are used in the biggest parade. Eventually, Old Spanish Days split into two organizations, and the carriages are now preserved by the Carriage Museum so they can emerge unscathed for their yearly trip up State Street.

*Santa Barbara's Carriage Museum houses 75 horse-drawn vehicles.*

There are approximately seventy-five wagons housed in a building with a modern adobe front on a wooden barn-like rear building. It's stuffed with mudwagons, freight wagons, passenger carriers, a covered army wagon, a hearse, and even a Spanish-festival wine cart dated to 1648. A long lineup of extremely fancy silver-inlaid saddles is on display, too.

The trustees act as docents, and they'll be happy to talk with you about their treasures. This museum is only about a block from the beach, near Santa Barbara's picturesque harbor. So if you're strolling around on a Sunday afternoon, it might be an interesting addition to your day. If it happens to be Sunday between 2 and 4 p.m., you could also visit Fernald House, the historic home operated by the Santa Barbara Historical Museum. Admission is $3 for adults, and it's only one short block from the Carriage Museum at 414 West Montecito Street.

**Hours:** 9 a.m. to 3 p.m. weekdays, 1 to 4 p.m. Sundays. Free admission, donations welcome.

**Directions:** From Stearns Wharf at the corner of State and Cabrillo, go north on Cabrillo to Castillo Street (a stoplight). Turn right, then left into the Pershing Park lot. You'll see the Carriage Museum at the back of the lot on the right side.

**Historical Document Display, 21 West Anapamu, Santa Barbara, 962-5322.** The Karpeles Manuscript Library owns over a million notable historical, literary, and scientific documents, making it the largest privately held significant manuscript collection in the world. In the library's fifty or so display cases, there is a revolving exhibit, which at any one time might include documents pertaining to the building of the Panama Canal and the exploration of the South Pole next to letters concerning the Mormon settlement of Utah. The conquest of South America by conquistadores might be reflected in other documents, along with some original Disney cartoon drawings and Egyptian hieroglyphs in sandstone.

Mr. Karpeles made his money in residential rental properties, and through his library he is giving some of it back by educating those who visit his eight museums across the U.S. He began collecting manuscripts in the late 1970s after seeing the Huntington Library's manuscripts, and his very first acquisition was a letter by H.G. Wells, writing about his confidence in the success of his upcoming *War of the Worlds.* Karpeles and his wife became fascinated with historical documents, and they continue to collect from around the world, often buying through auction houses such as Sotheby's. They feel that if one sees the actual documents that affected world change and growth, history will become much more real and personal. After a stop at their library, you'll probably agree with them.

Among their holdings are the 1865 Emancipation Proclamation amendment to the U.S. Constitution, and the proclamations and declarations of independence of Argentina and Peru. Mr. Karpeles has acquired manuscripts by early European royalty, along with writings by a number of famous literary figures like Mark Twain and Sir Arthur Conan Doyle. Sigmund Freud's work relating to dreams and many scientific works are there as well.

The manuscripts are lovingly displayed in a building Mr. Karpeles owns downtown, and visitors will find a multi-room exhibit facility there, with high ceilings and polished oak floors. You can call ahead to ascertain what is currently on display, but chances are that if you appreciate history, there will always be something to see that will arouse your interest.

**Hours:** 10 a.m. to 4 p.m. daily. Admission is free.

**Directions:** In Santa Barbara, State Street runs up from the ocean at Stearns Wharf, with address numbers going up from there. Anapamu Street intersects State between the 1100 and 1200 blocks, with the west addresses on the left and east addresses on the right (mountain) side, if you are heading away from the ocean. The library is one-half block off State. Parking lots downtown are located every block on Chapala and Anacapa streets, which both run parallel to State on either side of it. When trying to access a lot, just remember that turning left off of State Street during the day is prohibited.

*Vedanta Temple is a place of peace and tranquility.*

**Vedanta Temple/Sarada Convent Books, 925 & 927 Ladera Lane, Montecito, 969-5697.** For peace, tranquility, and a gorgeous ocean view, go to the Vedanta Temple. If you take East Valley Road heading south toward Ladera Lane, you'll be going through some interesting environs. This posh area with its lush foliage and rural atmosphere is home to many corporate titans and celebrities who prize Montecito for its privacy and beauty. Vedanta followers love the scenery too, but their lifestyle is the peaceful antithesis of the typical high-powered Montecito resident's.

The other-worldly Vedanta Temple was designed in 1956 by Lutah Maria Riggs, who had studied under the much-renowned architect George Washington Smith. Here Riggs departed from the Spanish-Colonial style Smith was known for to create a southern India-style masterpiece.

The temple grounds will make you feel as if you've entered a special, quiet space. The giant prayer bell, the well-done landscaping, and the sweeping views combine to signal serenity to the visitor. Upon entering the Sarada Convent Bookstore on the property, you'll find a good assortment of jewelry, greeting cards, cassette tapes, scarves, religious decorative items, and, of course, books. This is the most complete selection of non-Christian religious literature in the Santa Barbara area.

Vedanta is an offspring of the Ramakrishna Order of India, which was brought to the U.S. by Swami Vivekananda in 1893. The swami attended the World's Parliament of Religions in Chicago, and then remained in the States for three years. During this period, a number of Vedanta centers were founded. Their philosophy is basically that God exists in every being and that, in a sense, God is consciousness. Vedanta respects all religions, as they all are striving for the same goal, and the society welcomes visitors.

**Hours:** The bookstore is open Monday to Saturday, 10 a.m. to 5 p.m., and Sunday 10 a.m. to 1 p.m. Temple hours are 6:30 a.m. to 7:30 p.m. daily. Temple lectures are on Sunday mornings at 11 a.m.

**Directions:** From Santa Barbara go south on 101 to San Ysidro Road's exit. Turn left, and head toward the mountains. Turn right on East Valley Road, and drive to Ladera Lane. Turn left and watch for a small sign on the left side.

**The Blacksmith's Mansion, Montecito, 565-5653.** Casa del Herrero, or "House of the Blacksmith," was designed by the famed architect George Washington Smith for a very wealthy man named Steedman. Steedman was a silversmith who had made his fortune in the metal-manufacturing business in St. Louis, although he simply referred to himself as an "iron monger." During the '20s, the Steedmans scoured Spain and other European countries with a top-notch antiquarian in tow, looking for antique furniture, art, tiles, and architectural elements for their new home. Around the estate's eleven acres, noted landscape architects and horticulturalists, including the celebrated Lockwood de Forest, worked on the gardens. Here paths, fountains, and terraces were placed and walled gardens or "outside rooms" were created.

The Casa, although a large home by most people's standards, is a small Spanish-Moorish jewel when compared to many of the other grand Montecito estates. After Mr. and Mrs. Steedman died, their daughter, Medora Bass, inherited it, but because her husband's business was elsewhere, no family members lived at the estate for years. The gardens suffered, but fortunately the home was left exactly as is. Medora and her husband lived there in retirement for a few short years, and after their deaths, their son created the Casa del Herrero Foundation in 1993 to share this whimsical yet distinguished estate with the public.

Visitors will particularly appreciate the ceiling from a fifteenth-century convent that was built into the house, the little octagonal library, the tapestries, antiques, and artwork. A docent-led tour offers a true and amazing picture of how the wealthy lived in the '20s and '30s. Because the foundation is limited by the county to only 160 visitors per month, a reservation is mandatory, but planning ahead is worth it.

**Hours:** Tours are given on Wednesday and Saturday at 10 a.m. and 2 p.m., with alternate times occasionally available. Calling a couple of weeks ahead is often necessary, but if you want to book a tour within a day or two, call anyway. There may be a cancellation.

**Admission:** $10.00 per person.

**Directions:** Upon obtaining a reservation, get directions from the Casa del Herrero Foundation office.

*Goleta's old train depot has been resurrected as a railroad museum.*

**Train Station Without Tracks, 300 North Los Carneros Road, Goleta, 964-3540.** The original Goleta train station no longer sits next to tracks that lead someplace. It has been given new life and made into the South Coast Railroad Museum. Built in 1901, when the train first came through Santa Barbara on its way to points north, the building was moved in 1981 to a 140-acre county park. This feat was accomplished by the company that also moved the *Spruce Goose,* Howard Hughes' plane.

The building is surrounded by

golden fields, stately eucalyptus trees, and orchards. Nearby is a picnic area, and an old caboose adds to the ambience. Inside, you'll be taken back to the early 1900s. There's an old freight office where you can try your hand at Morse code, see typical office equipment of the day, and chat with friendly docent volunteers about railroad operations "back when." The passenger waiting room next door has a self-operated slide show of the moving and restoration of the depot. Their model railway exhibit, which uses Santa Barbara as a backdrop, could cause many a grown man to feel like a kid again, but if that doesn't do it, you may be lucky enough to hit a day when they're offering rides on their miniature railroad.

The depot shows railroad-related films on Thursday and Sunday; call for times and features. There's also a small, first-rate bookstore with a good selection of train posters and books on Santa Barbara history and lore. Perhaps the best time to visit is on weekend afternoons, when you can also tour the historic Stow House and the Sexton Museum next door.

**Hours:** 1 to 4 p.m., Wednesday through Sunday.

**Admission:** Free, donations welcome.

**Directions:** From Santa Barbara, go north on Hwy. 101 to the Los Carneros Road exit. Turn right, and shortly you'll see the depot on the right side of the road.

**Stow House, 304 North Los Carneros Road, Goleta, 964-4407.** Situated next door to the South Coast Railroad Museum, Stow House represents an even earlier day, when Goleta was an agricultural area and the only transportation was equine. The Stows were a very prosperous farm family, whose major crop was lemons. In fact, Goleta once produced one-tenth of the world's lemon crop, and the annual Lemon Festival is now held at Stow House every October.

This 1872 home was donated to the county in 1967, although Stow descendents still own orchards nearby. The Goleta Valley Historical Society spearheaded the restoration and furnishing of the property, and today you can view rich antique decor throughout its 5,000 square feet. Many of the items actually belonged to

*Stow House is a reminder of a slower, gentler age.*

the Stow family, and these have been augmented by other authentic period pieces. The property manager conducts tours on Saturday, with the perhaps more knowledgeable docents taking over on Sunday. Whoever takes you through the house should have some fun stories about the family's life in the home, especially if you ask good questions.

Outside, notice the many varieties of trees that were planted by the original residents, which now tower above the house. Nearby is the old red barn, housing the Horace Sexton Memorial Museum of farm implements and machinery, and a blacksmith shop, complete with blacksmiths hard at work.

This is an attraction that all ages can enjoy, especially since Lake Los Carneros is adjacent to the Railroad Museum and Stow House (see Lake Los Carneros, page 57).

**Hours:** 2 to 4 p.m., Saturday and Sunday. House tours are on the hour and half hour.

**Admission:** $3.00 donation suggested for the house tour. Grounds and Sexton Museum are free (donations are accepted).

**Directions:** See "Train Station Without Tracks" above.

**Where the Stagecoaches Stopped, 5995 Stagecoa Santa Ynez Valley, 967-0066.** Most people who have in Santa Barbara County have heard of Cold Spring Tav have even dropped by there on a weekend afternoon to hear the country or blues music and have a beer. The bar is an old log cabin, which once served as a bottling plant for natural spring water. Don't let the huge number of motorcyclists keep you from joining the afternoon crowd. Generally people from many walks of life are there, eating the delicious barbecued tri-tip sandwiches the tavern sells and enjoying the entertainment.

Cold Spring Tavern is situated in a wooded canyon, only a twenty-minute drive from Santa Barbara. If there were no automobiles around and the road wasn't paved, you could easily imagine you had stepped into a time warp. The tavern, its outbuildings, and grounds have been thoughtfully maintained to reflect their working past.

In the late 1800s, there was no railroad between Los Olivos and Santa Barbara. Mudwagons, which were stagecoaches outfitted for rough terrain, made the trip to connect the two rail lines. Passengers coming south started from Los Olivos, after most likely staying at Mattei's Tavern, which is still operating today as a

*Cold Spring Tavern was a respite for weary travelers then and a fun place to visit now.*

restaurant. From Santa Barbara, there is a series of signs marking the old stagecoach route. They stopped at Cold Spring Tavern for new horses, some food, and rest. The total trip, which now takes about forty-five minutes, took them eight hours, and it was a dusty, gruelling ride. To get an idea of what these passengers faced, you can see the mudwagon that made the very last run. It's on display at the Santa Barbara Carriage Museum (see page 19), and there are other examples at the Parks-Janeway Carriage House in Santa Ynez (see page 28). Audrey Ovington's family has owned the tavern since 1941, and her family has an interesting past of its own. Her father, Earl Ovington, was the famous aviator who made the first air-mail flight in history.

In an ivy-covered wooden building next to the bar, the restaurant's dinner menu runs the gamut from game meats to beef, fish, fowl, and vegetarian dishes. All dinners are $16, which includes soup and salad. It's good, but generally not for those who favor low-fat food. Be sure to make a reservation, and ask for the R.V. Room (*Rancheros Visitadores,* not recreational vehicle) to be near the rock fireplace. For weekend evenings, it wouldn't hurt to call several days ahead.

**Hours:** Lunch 11 a.m. to 3 p.m. daily. Dinner 5 p.m. to 9 p.m. Monday through Friday, until 10 p.m. on Saturday and Sunday. Live music on Saturday and Sunday afternoons and Friday evenings.

**Directions:** From Santa Barbara's 101, take 154/Cachuma Lake's exit. Proceed up 154 over San Marcos Pass. On the way down the pass, there is a small sign on the right for Stagecoach Road, but the next left is it. Once on Stagecoach, take the first right, which will head you down into Cold Spring's canyon.

**Cowboys and Carriages (and Indians), 3596 Sagunto Street, Santa Ynez, 688-7889.** The Santa Ynez Valley Historical Museum and the Parks-Janeway Carriage House have a perfect setting in the tiny western-style business district of Santa Ynez. A careful collection has been assembled, showcasing the area's Indian heritage and the days of the early American settlers. You can see everything from Indian basketry to western implements, firearms, photos, saddles, home furnishings, and clothing. There's also a reference library and a tiny gift shop.

On the other side of the courtyard is the Carriage Museum, which houses a fine display of thirty-eight horse drawn vehicles. They started collecting them in 1930, and they have everything from a covered wagon to a popcorn wagon. Lars Mortensen, the young and enthusiastic curator, has added an area at the back to house farm machinery, tools, and plows, and he has plans to make this museum even bigger and better as time goes on. Lars clearly loves this place. He says he waited years for the curator's position to open up, and he's never leaving.

**Hours:** Historical Museum 1 p.m. to 4 p.m., Friday through Sunday. Carriage Museum 9 a.m. to 4 p.m. Tuesday through Thursday, 1 p.m. to 4 p.m. Friday through Sunday. Donations are appreciated.

**Directions:** Follow directions to Solvang. After turning left onto Highway 246 but before Solvang, you'll pass the Santa Ynez Airport on the left. Turn right on Meadowvale. Follow its curve to the left, and it becomes Sagunto. The museum will be on your left.

**Olivas Adobe Historical Park, 4200 Olivas Park Drive, Ventura, 644-4346 or 658-4728.** The Olivas Adobe is hardly "off the beaten path." There are signs placed by the City of San Buenaventura pointing the way to this historic residence. Too many of us, however, tend to ignore California's monuments to yesteryear unless we're told that they really are worth a visit. If you're interested in adobe architecture, ranch life, or cowboys and Indians, you should see this two-story, gracious home.

Richard Senate, the site manager, has loads of stories about the rancho days, and about the Olivases and their twenty-one children. He has ways of making the second half of the 1800s come graphically alive. For instance, he calculates that if the same number of murders per capita were happening now as were committed back then, 250 people per day would be gunned down in cold blood. This was general lawlessness beyond our modern imaginations, and one of the benefits the Indians got for working

*The Olivas Adobe—a look at early California life.*

on the ranchos was protection from outlaws. Most ranchos paid little more than room and board, but Raymundo Olivas was generous. Each Indian family on his rancho was allowed to farm seven acres and keep 100 percent of their produce or sell it as they wished.

Olivas came to the area as a cavalryman at the Presidio at Santa Barbara. But after receiving his land grant from the Mexican governor, he made his fortune by selling beef to hungry gold miners up north. As Richard Senate is fond of saying, "He made it and he spent it." The Olivas family enjoyed such luxuries as ornate music boxes, French wallpaper, imported clothing, and smoked hams from Ireland. Remember, this was in the days before the airplane or the Panama Canal!

Don Raymundo Olivas now has over 2,000 direct descendents, but the last private owner of the Olivas home was Major Max Fleischmann, the yeast king who donated the funds for the building of Santa Barbara Harbor and new wings of Santa Barbara Cottage Hospital and the Natural History Museum, among other gifts. Fleischmann used the Olivas Adobe as a duck-hunting lodge, which must have been wonderful since the golf course next door was then marshland. His estate donated the Olivas Adobe to the City of Ventura to be used as an historic park, and many events are held there now, including summer concert telling nights, ghost tours, and fiestas. Movie companies used it as a location.

**Hours:** Grounds are open 10 a.m. to 4 p.m. daily, but make every effort to visit on Saturday or Sunday, when house tours are available. Admission is free, and donations are welcome.

**Directions:** From Santa Barbara, take 101 south to the Victoria Avenue exit in Ventura. Turn right on Victoria. You'll be going by an industrial park on your left. Stay in the right lane, and turn right on Olivas Park Drive. In approximately 1.25 miles, turn left into the Olivas Adobe grounds. It's the driveway after the one for PictSweet Mushroom Farm, the largest producer of mushrooms in California.

**Krotona, 2 Krotona Hill, Ojai, 646-2653.** Krotona is a theosophical establishment that is worth a drive-through for anyone who wishes to see panoramic views of the Ojai Valley. Those who are interested in philosophical or religious thought will want to stop at their bookshop, which features works on the world's religions, and area residents may borrow books and tapes from the library for a small annual membership fee.

Krotona is administrated by members of the very international Theosophical Society, which operates in over sixty countries. The society was founded in 1875 in New York City by a Russian woman and a man who was a veteran of the Civil War. They subsequently moved the society to India. Theosophy is not a religion. It embraces truths found in all religions and is dedicated to harmony among all people and the encouragement of the study of religion, philosophy, and science. Theosophy has attracted people as diverse as Thomas A. Edison, Jawaharlal Nehru, and William Butler Yeats.

The famous philosopher J. Krishnamurti focused and taught these ideals, and he made Krotona a base, in turn making Ojai more famous as a center for spiritual enlightenment. The lovely Spanish-style library is housed in his former home.

Founded in Hollywood in 1912, Krotona moved to Ojai in 1926 to provide a more spiritual atmosphere than was found in the budding movie capital, and now there is housing for students and visitors sprinkled around the 118-acre property. Krotona sponsors educational programs, and speakers such as Deepak Chopra and Jean Houston are presented here. You can call for information on upcoming events, or better yet, stop by.

**Hours:** Bookshop 11 a.m. to 5 p.m. Tuesday through Saturday, 1 to 5 p.m. Sunday. Library 10 a.m. to 5 p.m. Tuesday through Friday, 1 to 5 p.m. Saturday and Sunday.

**Directions:** From the intersection of routes 33 and 150, heading into Ojai on 150, turn left at Krotona's sign, approximately .10 of a mile past Villanova Preparatory School. It's the first left turn after you pass the Ojai city limit.

**Gallery of Historical Figures, McNell Road at Reeves Road, Ojai, 646-6574.** George Stuart worked at the Smithsonian Institution at one time, doing "as little as possible." He decided early in life that he wanted to be a "monologist," and ended up in Ojai by accident. A patron supported his activities as he began to create incredibly detailed human figures at a scale of three inches to the foot. These figures depict historical personages, and George calls them his "hook." People come to hear George's lectures so they can see these amazing human replicas.

George does all the work himself. He starts with the skeleton, and all joints are articulated. He builds the bodies from the inside out, and his anatomical knowledge must be extensive. Even the jewelry and clothing are created by George.

In 1967 or 1968 (George is not sure which), he opened his gallery in one end of his wonderful two-story Ojai farmhouse. Orange trees line one side of the house, a great stone wall another, and chickens wander around the yard. The gallery is one small room with a historical-period display of figures that changes quarterly. George plays music to match the figures being shown, and he'll be happy to talk with you about his activities.

George Stuart is a genuine character who's had somewhat of an unusual life. The day we visited, he was wearing all black. He appeared in his half-open Dutch front door, made sure we each gave our $1 donation, then let us inspect the gallery before appearing again. His figures are also on display at the Ventura County Historical Museum, where he is scheduled for three talks a month. When asked if his talks are any good, he responded that it depends on his audience. If they are boring, so is he. Call the museum at 653-0323 for information.

**Hours:** Open April to December, 1 to 4 p.m., Saturday and Sunday, or by appointment. $1 donation; closed when raining.

**Directions:** From downtown Ojai, go southeast on Ojai Avenue towards Santa Paula. At Boccali's Pizza, veer left onto Reeves Road. Turn left again onto McNell Road, and the Gallery is almost immediately on your left.

**Antique Aircraft Capital of the World, Santa Paula, 525-1109.** Santa Paula may not have the highest number of antique and exotic aircraft of any airport worldwide, but one visiting gentleman from Florida said, "This place is internationally famous. There must be fifty antique aircraft here!" Santa Paula is home to more stagger wings than almost anywhere else, and there are home-builts, experimental models, and everything from Aeroncas to Wacos.

The background of this airport is a story in itself. After the 1928 St. Francis Dam flood, which devastated the Santa Clara River Valley, river-side land came cheap. A rancher named Ralph

*Antique aircraft enthusiasts will love exploring Santa Paula Airport.*

Dickenson decided to sell twenty $1,000 shares, buy some property there, and start an airport. Today, the airport is still owned and managed by an association of shareholders. The corrugated-metal hangars are owned by private individuals who make land-lease payments to the association, and zip around the place in their golf carts. Pilots here talk among themselves via radio to decide who will land first, as there is no tower to control traffic.

The time to visit is the first Sunday of each month, during their open house. The docent station is near Logsdon's Restaurant, and you can get a free tour between 10 a.m. and 2 p.m., or you can "wing it." Many private hangars welcome visitors, car clubs may be exhibiting, and the seven hangars that house the Aviation Museum of Santa Paula will be showing their aircraft, cars, motorcycles, antiques, and memorabilia. Sightseeing flights are available, too, and these rides are FREE for kids from 9 to 17 through the Young Eagles program.

**Hours:** First Sunday of each month, 10 a.m. to 3 p.m. Summer months might be a little quieter, because more pilots are out of town.

**Directions:** 101 south to 126 toward Santa Paula. Exit at Palm Ave., Turn right, then left on Santa Maria St. There is no official airport parking, so park on the street near the hangars or by Logsdon's.

*Exhibits at the Unocal Oil Museum are inventive and informative.*

**Union Oil Museum, 1001 East Main Street, Santa Paula, 933-0076.** What could possibly be in an oil museum? Doesn't this sound dull? If you think so, think again. Unocal spent over $2 million to completely redo their museum, which is housed in their original 1890 Queen Anne brick-and-stone headquarters.

When you walk in, you'll be asked to clock in on their old fashioned timeclock, just like the oil workers did. Unocal has created colorful, eye-catching displays that include videos and even arcade-type games. You can play "Wildcatter," which shows you the odds drillers face when looking for oil, or watch old televison ads done by stars like Marilyn Monroe and Buster Keaton for Union Oil. There are areas that show Santa Paula's history, oil geology, oil production, and transportation. These displays are done in imaginative ways so that people of all ages can relate.

The Museum's pride and joy is their huge old cable-tool drilling rig, reassembled in a modern building at the rear. They have it running at a speed much slower than in the old days, when workers were in danger of losing fingers or worse from flying belts or cables. Now it's safe, and it's a fascinating look at antique machinery in motion.

**Hours:** Thursday through Sunday 10 a.m. to 4 p.m.

**Directions:** From Santa Barbara go south on 101. In Ventura, take Hwy. 126 to Santa Paula. Exit at the Tenth Street/Santa Paula exit, turn left, and go to Main Street. You'll see the historic museum building on the right side.

**Vintage Motorcycles and Motorcars, 1421 Emerson Avenue, Oxnard, 486-5929.** Hidden away in a 45,000-square-foot modern industrial building, *Los Angeles Times* publishing mogul Otis

*Early American, European, and Japanese motorcycles are collected by Otis Chandler and can be seen at his Vintage Museum.*

Chandler keeps his multi-million dollar Vintage Museum of Transportation and Wildlife, and every month or two when it suits him, he holds an open house. The rest of the time, he and his staff restore, tinker, and take various bikes out for a spin. Mr. Chandler does not operate his museum as a nonprofit institution, so he can do with it whatever he pleases.

Chandler used to have the largest collection of muscle cars in the world, but he got bored with them, and sold off all but a few gems. In their place, he has collected vintage motorcycles, and he now has one of the larger collections of antique American cycles in the world. He also has a Japanese and European motorcycle collection, which occupies the second floor.

Mr. Chandler does not have a one-track mind. He features 80 American classic cars, like the 1934 Packard Custom Town Car which was built for Jeannette MacDonald, a 1935 Auburn Speedster, a 1967 Corvette, and even an 1894 steam locomotive. Lining the walls are his big-game hunting trophies, which with today's sensibilities will not please every visitor to see, but one can certainly imagine the money it took to make all those hunting trips. For motorcycle enthusiasts, this group of over 130 rare bikes will make the trip worthwhile.

**Hours:** Call 486-5929 for the next open house date. Admission is $7.

**Directions:** From Santa Barbara take 101 south, exit at Rose Avenue. Turn left, go approximately 3 miles to Emerson and turn right. The building sign says "Vintage."

# Gardens, Growers, and Grapes

**Santa Barbara Winery, 202 Anacapa Street, Santa Barbara, 963-3633.** So you're in Santa Barbara and you'd like to do some wine tasting, but you don't have time to go to the Santa Ynez Valley? There's a solution. You won't see green rolling vineyards, but you will be able to participate in a winery tour that takes you through the entire viticultural process. More important, their winemaker, Bruce McGuire, puts out excellent wines for a $3 tasting fee.

Santa Barbara Winery is owned by Pierre LaFond, who is famed throughout the area for his Montecito and Santa Barbara gourmet shops/sidewalk cafes and his wife's upscale clothing stores called Wendy Foster. He owns a vineyard and also purchases grapes.

*Santa Barbara Winery has a convenient in-town tasting room.*

On tour, you'll see pictures of the grape-growing and harvesting process. This is quite an educational tour, and what Santa Barbara Winery lacks in atmosphere because the grapes aren't grown at the production facility, it makes up for with its friendly staff.

**Hours:** 10 a.m. to 5 p.m. daily. Tours are at 11:30 a.m. and 3:30 p.m., and last twenty minutes or more, depending on the number of questions asked. No reservations are required.

**Directions:** Anacapa Street runs parallel to State Street, one block south (actually east). The winery is at the corner of Anacapa and Yanonali streets, on the ocean side of 101.

**Orchids Galore, 1250 Orchid Drive, Santa Barbara, 967-1284.** The Santa Barbara Orchid Estate, situated in what most people think of as Goleta, is approached through an area of other large commercial nursery operations. The front entry of the Estate has a large lawn area, but don't expect a park-like setting. The owners are more interested in growing world-class orchids than they are in having a showplace.

The Gripp family has been involved with the Orchid Estate since 1957. They host one of the most important orchid fairs in the world the third weekend of each July, which is attended by many international growers. The Estate also has a special open house the same weekend as the Orchid Show at Earl Warren Showgrounds in March or April, and another one in November. The best time to visit is actually anytime from February to May, when the cymbidiums are in bloom. They grow more than 2,000 varieties, including the popular cattleya and phalaenopsis, and they sell their orchids both as plants and as cut flowers.

When you visit, you'll be allowed to walk through the one-acre glass-covered lath house where the cymbidiums are grown and through smaller greenhouses where other varieties are kept. At the end, an outdoor sales area may tempt you, and salespeople can answer all your questions. If you don't want to buy a plant for yourself, you may want to have one of their orchid gift boxes sent to your mother or a special friend (January through May).

If you haven't had enough of orchids after your visit, Stewart

Orchids at 3376 Foothill Road in Carpinteria also welcomes the public, 684-5448, also Gallup & Stribling Orchids, 684-9842.

**Hours:** 8 a.m. to 4:30 p.m., Monday through Saturday. 11 a.m. to 4 p.m. Sunday.

**Directions:** From Santa Barbara take 101 north to the Patterson exit. Turn left. You will see nurseries after you pass Goleta Valley Hospital. Patterson Avenue curves and eventually becomes Orchid Drive. Orchid goes into a residential neighborhood, where Santa Barbara Orchid Estate is located on the left side of the road.

**Conservation on Display, 930 Miramonte Drive, Santa Barbara, 963-0583.** Hidden away on a hilltop with gorgeous views of Santa Barbara is a well-planned exercise in energy conservation and organic gardening. The Gildea Resource Center is operated by the Community Environmental Council, which was founded after Santa Barbara's disastrous 1969 oil spill. The Center and its adjacent garden building employ just about every method of natural energy. There is a printed self-guided tour to show the visitor the sod roof, photovoltaic arrays that turn sunlight into electricity, composting toilets, building orientation to best use natural light and warmth, solar hot water pumps, rain water collection, and so on. For anyone interested in ecologically sound building methods, this should be an educational visit.

Outside, their large demonstration garden boasts a mixture of flowers and vegetables and an orchard and drought-tolerant landscaping. Anyone can become a volunteer gardener here, and in the process learn about composting and organic gardening.

The CEC is involved in a variety of environmental projects, and it is a good source of information on recycling, hazardous waste, and safe alternatives to pesticide use and hazardous household products. Take the self-guided tour anytime during business hours, or if you have a specific interest, call ahead for a guided tour. The CEC also operates an interesting Watershed Resource Center near Arroyo Burro Beach.

**Hours:** 9 a.m. to 5 p.m., Monday through Friday. No admission charge.

**Directions:** From downtown, go west on Carrillo. Heading up the hill, turn left on Miramonte Drive. At the far end of the Highlands condominiums, turn left down the Gildea Resource Center's driveway, which it shares with the condos. For parking, it might be better to leave your car on Miramonte, as the Center's parking is limited.

**Pick Your Own Oranges, Goleta, 968-1162.** If you like to squeeze your own juice, this is the place. But if you don't, go to the Ellwood Ranch anyway. They just might have avocados or something else for sale, too. The scenery is quintessential California, and getting there almost feels like an adventure.

The Ellwood Ranch is at the outer reaches of Goleta. Approaching the entrance, you'll see an area in transition from rural to residential. Once on the ranch, though, you'll be driving through orange groves and beautiful chaparral canyons, and you'll see the Doty's reservoir and sand and topsoil supply yard.

At the you-pick orange grove you may meet John Doty, one of the ranch family members. He began the self-serve operation in 1969, when the cost of farm labor was higher than the price of oranges. People have been coming ever since to scoop up his sweet crop at $3 per bucket, and he'll be happy to tell you the location of the best picking.

If you're interested in ranching, talk with Mr. Doty about it. He's lived on the ranch since 1920, except for one short period in San Francisco, and he headed right back to the ranch. He'll tell you about what it was like to be a kid there, and the problems ranchers face these days, and you'll come away enriched after meeting someone in a different walk of life. You'll also have some inexpensive, tasty food to take home.

**Hours:** 9 a.m. to 5 p.m. daily from July 1 until the crop is gone, sometime between November and January. Call before going to the ranch, just in case the Dotys haven't been able to staff the grove that day, and if there is a closed sign at the gate, please respect it.

**Directions:** From Santa Barbara take Highway 101 north to the Winchester Canyon Road exit. Turn right onto Winchester

Canyon Road, and at Cathedral Oaks Road turn right again. Take the next left onto Ellwood Canyon Road. Going up this road, stay right where the sign says "ORANGES, SAND." Go to the left (downhill) to reach the ranch gate. You will see a sign that says "1100 SANTA BARBARA SAND" where you turn left into Ellwood Ranch. Follow the ranch road: it curves to the right, then goes straight. There is an orchard on your right, then the truck yard with a chainlink fence around it. Following that is a gray house with an apparently abandoned dairy barn and eventually a sign saying "1205." Just before this sign, a road veers down to the right, which will lead you to the picking grove. It is approximately 1.4 miles from the ranch gate to the grove, and most of it is paved. It can be dusty there, but even if you have to wash your car afterward, the trip is worth it.

**Sunstone Vineyards and Winery, 125 Refugio Road, Santa Ynez, 688-WINE.** The Rice family has been in residential real estate development over the years, but they took a new direction in 1994 when they opened their charming winery. Their residence is also located on the property, and they've already created the air of a long-established French Provençal vineyard.

After driving between Sunstone's oak trees and vineyards, visitors park and pass through a vine-covered arch to find a Mediterranean courtyard "to die for." White market umbrellas shade tables made of wine barrels, surrounded by plantings of lavendar, rosemary, and geraniums. The winery building was built to seem ancient, with ocher-colored walls and a covered stone porch. Inside, the tasting room and cave await. Merlot is their signature wine, but several other varietals are also available. This winery is so lovely that it's hard to go back to the real world. Take your time.

**Hours:** 10 a.m. to 4 p.m. daily. $3 per person for tasting, including souvenir glass.

**Directions:** 101 north, exit at 154/Cachuma Lake. Take 154 over San Marcos Pass. Turn left on Highway 246, then left on Refugio Road (a stoplight). Sunstone is approximately 1.4 miles down Refugio Road, past Santa Ynez Winery. Watch for their entrance sign, just before the Santa Ynez River.

*Both kids and adults love watching Quicksilver's tiny horses.*

**Quicksilver Miniature Horse Farm, 1555 Alamo Pintado Road, Solvang, 686-4002.** Some people have kidded that miniature horses may someday replace dogs as man's best friend because they help keep the grass cut and they don't bark. With their high price tags, we doubt it, but they're so cute that they're hard to resist.

Miniature horses were originally bred to pull ore carts in English mines, because larger ponies wouldn't fit in the shafts. These little guys can pull up to ten times their weight, and unlike Shetlands, they have a sweet disposition. If they get to be over 34 inches tall from the base of the mane to the floor, they no longer qualify as miniatures, and there's an association that regulates the breed and oversees shows.

Quicksilver Ranch, in between Solvang and Los Olivos, is one of the West's major miniature horse breeders. It's owned by the Stribling family, who are known for their huge orchid growing facility in Carpinteria. As miniature horses become better known as a breed, they are bigger and bigger business. One tiny horse can cost from $2,500 to $10,000, depending on whether it is "pet quality" or a show horse.

Business aside, one gets the feeling that the Striblings have this ranch because of the delight they take in their animals. The fenced pastures and barn are pristine, and the barnstalls have everything a horse could want. There are even television monitors, so that mothers-to-be can be watched twenty-four hours a day and be given help when they need it. April and May are the busiest months for delivering newborns. These minis have it made. They've got a luxurious home, people to take care of their every desire, and an adoring public.

**Hours:** 10 a.m. to 3 p.m. daily.

**Directions:** See directions to Solvang. The second stoplight you'll hit on 246 is Alamo Pintado Road. Turn right, and watch the addresses. The ranch is on the left side of the road, up maybe a mile or so.

**Gazebo by the Lake with Winery Attached, 2670 Ontiveros Road, Los Olivos, 688-8664.** Beckmen Vineyards is just slightly off the beaten winery track, but it's worth the detour. The Beckmen family bought the property from Dave and Margy Houtz in 1994, after Tom Beckmen sold his company, Roland Corp. U.S., which manufactured electronic musical instruments. Since then they've

*The Beckmen Vineyards' gazebos are the perfect place to picnic.*

made improvements to their wine-making facility, the wines' quality, and their extremely charming picnic area.

Tom spends part-time here, but his son Steve oversees day-to-day winery operations and works with wine consultant Jeff Newton to produce their fine wines. They've put a lot of work into improving the grape production of the vineyards, and have recently planted eight acres of syrah and merlot grapes.

Visit Beckmen as much for the scenery as for the wine. Approaching the entrance on Ontiveros Road, you'll go by a long row of apple trees, with vistas beyond of vineyards and farms, rolling golden hills and blue sky. While you're there, you'll feel like you're on a farm, and in fact, the tasting is done near the barn. Please do avail yourself of one of three gazebo picnic areas overlooking their duck pond. The Santa Ynez Valley offers many great picnic sites, but this is one of the most idyllic, so go armed with goodies. At the winery, you can buy one of their varietal wines to complete the meal.

**Hours:** 11 a.m. to 5 p.m., Friday through Sunday. Summer open daily. $2.50 tasting fee.

**Directions:** Take 101 north to 154 San Marcos Pass/ Cachuma Lake exit. Go straight through the light, then the road curves left. Follow it to the first light, turn right and you'll be on 154. Go over the pass, by Lake Cachuma, and turn left on Roblar Avenue (stay on 154 beyond the turnoff for 246/ Solvang). Just past Refugio Road, Ontiveros Road veers off of Roblar. From the Ontiveros Road sign, follow the signs for the winery, which will take you to their entrance.

**Rancho Sisquoc Winery, Foxen Canyon Road, Santa Maria, 934-4332.** Because Rancho Sisquoc isn't very close to the popular tourist areas of Santa Barbara, many wine enthusiasts miss it, thereby passing up a lovely little picnic spot and a chance to drive through Western-looking private cattle ranch land.

From Santa Barbara, the drive is fetchingly scenic, going through mountains and rolling golden hills, by ranches and the other wineries of the Foxen Canyon Wine Trail. You can stop in Los Olivos and visit the art galleries on the way. Foxen Canyon

*The trip to Rancho Sisquoc is a rewarding sidetrip.*

Road is never crowded, and you'll feel like you've really "gotten away," even though the drive to Rancho Sisquoc takes only a little over an hour. Foxen Canyon Road was named after an English sea captain who owned an entire Spanish rancho; he was accused of collaborating with the invading Americanos in 1846, but that is another story.

Rancho Sisquoc is owned by the Flood family of San Francisco, known for the wealth they gained through mining the Comstock Lode. They don't live on the ranch, but they keep it active, with cattle being their main business. There are 37,000 acres of property, and only 300-plus acres are planted with grapes, but it's the second oldest vineyard in Santa Barbara County, illustrating that the county's wine industry is quite new. Their first vintage was in 1972, and production is still fairly small.

When you turn off Foxen Canyon Road into the ranch, you'll go for almost two miles before reaching the winsome little wooden winery. Even during the dry season, the area around the winery building is kept green and inviting, and you are welcome to use their picnic tables. With a busy highway nowhere near, this is a great escape from the high-tech real world.

**Hours:** 10 a.m. to 4 p.m. daily. Tasting charge only for groups of ten or more.

**Directions:** See directions to Los Olivos (page 73). Go straight on 154 past Grand Avenue, and turn right on Foxen Canyon Road. When you reach the intersection where you must turn right or left, turn right. Continue past Parker Winery and Zaca Mesa Winery. At the small white 1875 country church on the right, which one of Foxen's daughters had built of wood boated south from Redwood City, you'll see the Rancho Sisquoc sign. Turn right into the ranch, and watch for a sign to the winery building.

**Lompoc Flower Fields.** Everyone who has lived in Santa Barbara County for a while has heard of Lompoc's legendary expanses of blooms, but how many people have gone to see them? This is a major industry that deserves a look. The flower-seed business started here in the early part of this century, when one bean farmer decided to grow some sweet peas. A bean seed buyer from Burpee Seeds saw the sweet peas and that was the beginning of one of Lompoc's major industries. Today the Bodger and Pan American seed companies dominate the valley, which is approximately twelve miles long and three miles wide. Because it is shaped like a funnel, it draws wind and fog. These factors are important in flower-seed production—wind because it allows pollination and fog because of its moderating affect on the climate.

From May through July the seed companies put on a show for everyone to see. Then veritable carpets of color cross the landscape. Plants are transplanted from greenhouse flats to the fields and grow there until the seeds are harvested. Present in large quantities are snapdragons, pansies, poppies, delphinium, gazanias, petunias, sweet peas, marigolds, and on and on.

The height of the season is usually in June, when Lompoc holds its Flower Festival during the last full weekend. The Lompoc Chamber of Commerce is a source of festival information at 736-4567. If you are interested in touring a greenhouse operation, Bodger Seeds is open for two weeks in April each year. For a small charge, which benefits the Lompoc Beautification Commission, visitors can see a video on seed production, then take a self-guided walk through the facility. Call the City Trees Department at 736-1261 for information on this tour.

There is some etiquette involved in flower-field ogling. The growers ask that you keep your vehicle on paved roads so that the dust doesn't harm the flowers' growth. Also, because the fields are private property, please don't walk in them or pick the flowers. Other than that, they just want you to enjoy the results of their efforts. The results are huge. Lompoc area growers get anywhere from 30 to 800 pounds of seed per acre, depending on the flower variety, and they produce more than half the world's flower seeds.

If you're wondering what else you can do to justify a sidetrip to Lompoc, so that you have a nice stopping point, consider the La Purísima Mission State Park, just outside Lompoc on Purísima Road. It is one of the most interesting missions of the entire California chain, with indoor and outdoor displays of mission life, gardens, and even a picnic area. There's a small admission charge of $5 per car. It's a beautiful place, as well as being entertaining and educational. On the way home, consult this book for other spots you might want to include on your tour.

**Directions to the flower fields:** Go north on 101. Take the Highway 1 turnoff to Lompoc, and follow it. You will drive through San Julian Ranch, one of the original Spanish land grant ranchos. At Ocean Avenue turn left, and go through Lompoc. At V Street you'll start seeing flowers. Continue to DeWolfe Avenue, turn right, and go to Central Avenue. Turn right again and you'll be headed back toward town. If you want to go to La Purísima Mission, turn left off Central onto H Street, and right on La Purísima Road.

**Salt Marsh Nature Park, Carpinteria, 893-4127.** There's still a place in the Santa Barbara vicinity where you can experience a piece of California's coastal wetland. It's surrounded by houses and a mobile home park, but at over 200 acres, you'll get a good feel for what has been lost elsewhere. California only retains about ten percent of the wetlands it originally had, and the University of California Natural Reserve System is making sure that here, at least, development will go no further.

Their work in Carpinteria began in 1977, when they bought a portion of the marsh. Now the City of Carpinteria owns eight acres along Ash Avenue, which is part of the 230 acre preserve administrated by UC. These eight acres have been turned into a nature park, with paths, a boardwalk, interpretive signs, and native plantings. To the casual observer, this "park" is not an aesthetic paradise, but there's a lot going on here if you pay attention. To make it easier, you can attend a free docent-led tour any Saturday at 10:00 a.m. at the corner of Ash and Sandyland.

This marsh is a natural purifying system. It's been re-attached to the ocean tides and to fresh water flows, as it was before man intruded earlier in the twentieth century. Now halibut use it as a hatchery site, and other fish and crabs visit the marsh as well. Birds love this peaceful, safe wetland, and a number of endangered species have been sighted there. Depending on the season, you may see ducks and shorebirds, egrets, herons, osprey and eagles, sandpipers or raptors. Beyond the nature park's paths and walkways is off limits, but if you really want to get into the marsh, call Andy Brooks, the reserve's director. He leads tours of the reserve by appointment for those who are really interested.

**Hours**: Open daily.

**Directions:** Going south on 101, exit at Linden Avenue in Carpinteria. Turn right, and near the ocean turn right on Sandyland Avenue. Park near the corner of Sandyland and Ash.

**New Age Nature Walk to Self Discovery, Ojai, 646-2000.** "I call this walk 'inner-tainment,'" Zubin explains, describing the contemplative, labyrinthian trail he has carved through the high chaparral on his eighteen-acre "Studio of the Hills" property above Ojai. He worked from 6:00 a.m. to 1:00 p.m. daily for six months to clear his little "path to personal enlightenment" and furnish it with props to make the walker stop and think. He delights in sharing it with the public through the Inspirit Foundation, which he started with his wife, Shahastra, but he cautions that "The Walk" is best done alone or as a couple, not in a larger group.

Earlier in Zubin's career, he was a dancer and creator of tie-dye techniques, while Shahastra was a jeweler, ceramicist, and

painter. Currently, their hearts seem to be still in the sixties peace, love and self-expression movement, but they've tapped into the big money convention business. They market their engraved stone and wrought iron signs, and iron human figures to hotel chains, for use at group functions. Shahastra's whimsical figures are based on Zubin's dance movements, and they hold one or more food bowls. Zubin claims it's the first innovation in food presentation in fifty years.

Driving up to the Studio of the Hills feels like an adventure. You'll go up the side of the Topa Topa Mountains, and pass a couple of trailheads. Once parked, you walk by the house, the wrought iron show area, and the multi-level stage where the Foundation offers occasional poetry, music and dance performances. Then it's into the canopy of the tall chaparral, to begin this unique interactive experience.

Wooden carved hands point the way to eighteen sites in the woods, where the walker is invited to rediscover nature and reflect on life. The distance is short, but most people take about one hour to complete it. We won't spoil all the surprises along the way, but a few of the stops include poetry, making your own music, and writing inscriptions. Shahastra's stone plaques appear on the path periodically, with new age-style sayings like, "Listen to the song of your soul." When you emerge from the woods, there is a geodesic dome tent for relaxing or meditating, if you wish, before returning to the real world. Their guest book contains comments like "Always magical," and "A true oasis."

Zubin estimates that 3,000 people have taken "The Walk" since 1999, and most of them have found it by word of mouth. He hopes it will inspire others to create similar experiences in other places. One of his friends commented, "I've never seen another walk like this one, although there may be one somewhere. But there's definitely no one like Zubin."

**Hours:** By appointment only, 646-2000 or e-mail TheWalk@aol.com. Suggested donation $10 per person, to be placed in the bird house at the walk's start. But if you can't afford anything, you are still welcome.

**Directions:** When you make an appointment, you will be given directions. Please make note: (1) Their directions say to turn left on their road about two miles OUT of Ojai, but it is basically where town ends. If you get to Boccali's Pizza (on the left), you've gone way too far. (2) Their mailbox with 2150 on it is hard to spot. Be aware that they share a driveway with 2525, which is easier to see.

**Old Creek Ranch Winery, 10024 Old Creek Road, Oak View, 649-4132.** What is it about visiting wineries that is so much fun? Exercising one's love of the grape? That's part of it, but there's also that small thrill of discovery when you stumble on a site that evokes feelings of indulgence, leisure, and beauty. Old Creek Ranch Winery is one such place.

The ranch is located in an area better known for its citrus than its vineyards, but here several varietals are produced, and the ranch has a long history of wine making. The Rivas family owned the property for eighty years, and they produced wine for most of that time. The ruins of their winery are right behind the present-day tasting room. The story goes that during Prohibition customers would leave their wine order hanging on the Rivas's clothesline, with a basket of maybe bread or vegetables to trade. They would come back later and their wine would be waiting under the tree.

Mike and Carmel Maitland purchased the ranch while he was a vice president at MCA Records. Today the winery is run by

*Old Creek Ranch Winery produces modern vintages at a historic ranch site.*

their daughter and son-in-law, who don't live there, but visit often to oversee operations. They depend on the Maitlands' original winemaker, Chuck Branham, who is also a high school science teacher. He uses his scientific knowledge to produce award-winning premium wines, made from both the ranch's production and purchased grapes.

When you arrive, you'll be treated to the sight of a farm completely surrounded by hills. Horses nibble away at the undulating fields, and beyond are the vineyards. You'll see their antique farm equipment, and have an opportunity to try the wines, and make use of their deck for a picnic.

**Hours:** 11 a.m. to 5 p.m. weekends. Tasting fee.

**Directions:** From Santa Barbara, take 101 south, then 150 to Ojai. At the junction of 150 and Highway 33, turn right toward Ventura and Oak View. Turn left on Old Creek Road, which runs along the side of the Rancho Arnaz fruit stand. Follow Old Creek Road all the way to the end to find the winery.

# Green Places

**Elings Park, 1298 Las Positas Road, Santa Barbara, 569-5611.** Sitting on a former landfill, Elings Park is now Santa Barbara's largest park, at 230 acres. It is the site of over 2,800 softball and soccer matches every year and has areas for dirt biking and paragliding. Casual visitors probably won't get involved in any of these activities, but perched on the hill above the playing fields are several picnic areas and benches for their use, with magnificent views of the city and ocean.

All these facilities are here thanks to a very hard-working group of Santa Barbarans who have donated incredible amounts of time and raised millions of dollars. The park is operated by a nonprofit foundation, which is working on further improvements, including a more official entry to the South Park area. This property, which has been used for years by hang gliders and paragliders, was purchased from the Jesuits at a greatly discounted price. Eventually, there will be more family picnic areas on the South Park hill, but visitors are welcome to go up there now for the views or to watch the paragliders.

Godric Grove and Singleton Pavilion are the largest picnic event areas in the park and are usually reserved by large parties on weekends. Going there on a weekday evening, however, would usually allow a choice of sites, including Godric Grove's wonderfully charming, oak-shaded deck with round picnic tables and a great city view. Late afternoons, you may also see remote-control gliders being flown from this hill, near the Veterans Memorial.

If you want some exercise, take the short steep trail that goes to the left, where a small sign points to a nature and jogging trail to the right. It starts on the main park road, just below the park office, and you'll go up to South Park. At the top, there's a ridge with city views, and if you walk around the farmer's fields beyond, you'll reach the parking area for paragliders. If you're lucky, you may get to watch a paragliding lesson (see page 91), or see the red-tailed hawks soar.

**Hours:** Basically, the park closes at sunset. Officially, for rental purposes, the hours are 8 a.m. to sunset daily.

**Directions:** From 101, exit at Las Positas, and go toward the ocean on Las Positas Road. After passing the tennis courts on the left, watch for the park's stone entryway on the left.

In the park, go up the hill past the playing fields, and go left at the park office and parking lot. Continue up the hill to reach the picnic and view areas.

If you wish to visit the paragliding area without hiking up a hill, do not turn left into the park's entrance. Instead, continue on Las Positas to Cliff Drive, and turn left. About one block up Cliff Drive, there is a wider dirt area on the left with a metal fence blocking the dirt road going up the hill. If it's open, that means the paragliders are there. Bear left at each junction going up the hill to reach the parking area.

The very experienced and gracious instructors love to have visitors.

**Preserve on the Ocean Bluffs, Santa Barbara.** That this 70-acre open space exists at all is a monument to the determination of Santa Barbarans to save their remaining wilderness areas, especially this last 2,300 feet of undeveloped ocean frontage. With a history of being used by the public for walking, biking, hang gliding, and watching the sunset, there was no way locals would let "The Wilcox" be built upon without a fight.

The property had been used by Roy Wilcox as a wholesale nursery until the early 1970s, and remnants of his operation, like birds of paradise and eugenia, can still be seen. Sixteen heirs held the land after he passed away, but in 1985 it was sold to local developers for $4.5 million. They proposed more than one type of development, but in each case either approval or financing was lacking. Tired of fighting, the developers actually donated $90,000 to support a measure that would have allowed the city to buy the property from them. But bond measures in 1987 and 1988 requiring a two-thirds majority narrowly failed.

The property sat on the market at $7 million, but with the developers' equity eroded to nothing, their lender agreed in 1996 to sell the property to a preservation group for $3.5 million. The group's fund raising went into high gear, and between government grants, Coastal Resource Enhancement Funds, and private donations from school kids' allowance money to an anonymous $600,000 gift, they made it.

In December 1996, on the actor Kirk Douglas's eightieth birthday, the anonymous donor went public. He was Kirk's son, actor Michael Douglas. Michael, a Montecito resident, was granted the right to name the property, and he did so in honor of his father.

This is not a park. There are no restrooms, no paved walkways, and no flower beds. The Douglas Family Preserve will be left in its natural state, a flat grassy mesa with cypress, live oaks, eucalyptus, and native shrubs. Red-tailed hawks, seagulls, green-backed herons and belted kingfishers fly overhead, and in winter monarch butterflies roost in the eucalyptus. Now visitors will be allowed to stroll and enjoy the property's ragged splendor forever.

**Directions:** From Highway 101 take the Las Positas Road exit, and follow Las Positas toward the ocean all the way to Cliff Drive. If you're in the mood for an uphill walk, you can go straight across Cliff Drive, and park in the dirt pull-out (you'll see a yellow fire hydrant here). Follow the trail up the hill through the trees. For a flat approach, from Las Positas turn left on Cliff, right on Mesa Lane, right on Burton Drive, and left on Linda Road. Park near the end in the 300 block and go through the metal gate near the border of eucalyptus trees.

**Picnic Table with a View, Santa Barbara.** Maybe you didn't manage to get a room with a view when you rented your hotel room or bought your house. You can compensate at a couple of hidden parks in Santa Barbara that offer exquisite vistas, free for the looking.

• **Hilda McIntyre Ray Park** is one of the least known ones in the Santa Barbara system. At the end of a residential street on the Mesa, Mrs. McIntyre's former homesite is a downward-sloping, undulating lawn, dotted with gnarled live oak trees. The view here is sweepingly panoramic from all spots in the park, looking out over the city and the Santa Ynez Mountains. There are several picnic tables with barbecue pits, alcohol is permitted for the adults, and play equipment is provided for kids.

• **Franceschi Park** is on the other side of town, sitting up on the Riviera. This was also a former residence, occupied by one of the area's foremost horticulturalists. Unlike Ray Park, the home is still standing, awaiting funding for rehabilitation. Dr. Franceschi had an extensive Mediterranean garden and was responsible for bringing over 1,200 foreign plants to the United States. In fact, Franceschi and three other Santa Barbara men are often credited with changing the California skyline through their furtherance of botanical interest among the general public.

The story of the garden is that for ten years after Franceschi's death, the caretaker was an ex-boxer. While he knew all the Latin plant names, that was the extent of his gardening expertise, and the property quickly deteriorated. It's still pretty, though overgrown, and different plants have taken over from what the original owner had chosen. A few of them are labeled, and there are a couple paths winding to the house and along the hillside garden for the curious. Eventually, the local Horticultural Society hopes to make this spot once again a horticulturally significant center.

This is a tiny park, consisting mainly of a smallish patio with two picnic tables, framed by eucalyptus trees and graced with an incredible view of the city, ocean, and islands. There is no lawn and no play area. Franceschi is simply a premier spot to sneak away to for a romantic picnic, or to toast the sunset with your favorite nonalcoholic beverage.

**Hours:** Both parks are open from sunrise to one-half hour after sunset.

**Directions to Ray Park:** From downtown, go west on Carrillo Street, under the freeway and up the hill. Turn right on Mountain View, then veer right on Kenwood Road, which curves.

Follow the Kenwood Road signs to the park, which is across the street from 1427 Kenwood.

**Directions to Franceschi Park:** Riviera roads follow the winding old cowpaths and are sometimes hard to decipher for visitors, so what follows is the easiest "scenic route." From downtown, head up State to Los Olivos, and turn right. Drive past the Mission, veering right onto Alameda Padre Serra (you'll see a sign for El Encanto, a great place for a drink in elegant surroundings overlooking the city). Go left on Lasuen at the next El Encanto sign, then take the first left again up the hill. Turn right on Mission Ridge Road. You'll eventually pass a sign for Franceschi Park on the left. Turn left up Franceschi Road, then left into the park gates. Past the old house on your left there is a parking area above the patio. Please note that alcohol is not allowed.

**Lake Los Carneros, Goleta.** If you're looking for peace and quiet or if you would like to visit one of Santa Barbara's premiere birding locations, head for Lake Los Carneros. This twenty-two acre freshwater lake is part of a 140-acre county-owned preserve, and it has been known to harbor 220 different bird species. Some of the birds you may observe include coots, herons, egrets, cormorants, hawks, and owls. There are a variety of waterfowl and songbirds, and several species of warm-water fish inhabit the lake. Early-morning visitors may spot wildlife as well, such as foxes, coyotes, and raccoons.

You'll see the native scrub and wetland vegetation, as well as eucalyptus, pines, and other trees that were planted when this was part of the Stow Ranch. But the Stows weren't the first people here. Evidence of human use of this area can be traced back at least 9,000 years. Water has always been an issue in modern-day California, and it was essential to our ancestors as well, who lived off of the lake's fish and water fowl, water-loving mammals, and plants.

From the lake, there are beautiful views of the Santa Ynez Mountains, and if you keep following the trail, you'll eventually cross a wooden walkway over a reed-filled end of the lake. Lake Los Carneros is one of those accessible bits of nature that you can zip through in half an hour or take chairs and a picnic and spend a few hours painting, birdwatching, reading, or just plain relaxing.

**Hours:** 8 a.m. to sunset.

**Directions:** You can reach the lake from two sides. From the back yard of Stow House (see page 25) near the entrance to the Sexton Museum, a path leads to the lake. Just after the trail starts, if you go left down the hill through the vegetation on a dirt path, you'll access the wooden walkway, or you can stay on the main path. Alternatively, from Santa Barbara take Highway 101 north to the Fairview exit. Go right, but get immediately in the left lane, and turn left on Calle Real. Turn right on La Patera, go approximately two blocks, and you'll see a white metal fence on the left side of the road (across from 150 La Patera). This is the preserve's entrance.

**Santa Barbara Cemetery, East Cabrillo Boulevard and Channel Drive, Santa Barbara.** One of Santa Barbara's most delightful places to walk isn't a park, a beach, or a trail. It's the final resting place of many prominent Santa Barbarans, including the actor

*Santa Barbara Cemetery—a delightful place for a stroll.*

Ronald Coleman. Locals have been known to joke that it is some of the most expensive real estate per square foot in a town known for its already high real estate values.

The cemetery is located just across the street from the Andree Clark Bird Refuge, on a knoll that ends at the cliffs overlooking the Pacific. From the top of the hill, the views are stunning. The Santa Ynez mountain range is on one side, the ocean on the other. If that isn't enough, there are marble temples, rough-hewn stone mausoleums, and even a large pyramid to inspect. Among the flat grave stones there's a military section, and even an area where every marker has an engraved motorcycle on it.

Sturdy cyprus trees, exotic palms, and flowers ornament the property. The Moorish building with the blue-tiled dome and red-tile roof was designed by the famous architect, George Washington Smith, in 1926. Inside, there's a chapel containing noteworthy frescoes by Mexican artist Alfredo Ramos Martinez.

Bicycles and motorcycles are not allowed inside the cemetery. However, since the beach bike path brings you right to the cemetery entrance, this is a perfect place to stop on a bike ride and take a scenic stroll.

**Hours:** 8 a.m. to 5 p.m. daily, slightly shorter hours for the chapel building.

**Directions:** At State Street and Cabrillo Boulevard, facing Stearns Wharf, go left on Cabrillo. Continue past the East Beach volleyball courts and around the Bird Refuge. Veer right where Cabrillo splits toward the end of the Bird Refuge and you will curve onto Channel Drive. The entrance to the cemetery is on your right. An alternate route is to take Hwy. 101 to the Hot Springs Road exit. Turn toward the ocean, then left on Channel Drive.

**Montecito's Enchanted Forest, 1730 San Leandro Lane, Montecito.** Graceful old stone bridges spanning a burbling creek, ancient oak trees, peeks of hidden-away mansions, a eucalyptus forest where monarch butterflies roost, and the sight of a historic old adobe await those who want to take a nature walk in Santa Barbara's most prestigious "suburb." Thanks to developers who were more environmentally sensitive than some, this forty-four acre preserve is now administered by the Land Trust and open to the public, at least to those who can find it.

The preserve is part of the old Boeseke estate, which has a rather glamorous past and a more glitzy present, since part of the estate has been developed into luxury homes. The large historic adobe in the middle of the property occupies a sweeping green knoll, with hundred-year-old olive trees lining the approach. It was built in 1845 by a Spanish soldier named Domínguez, who was given a land grant by the Mexican government. His family farmed the ranch for many years, and then during the 1870s and 1880s the ranch changed hands more than once, passing into American hands.

The heyday of grand estate building in Montecito (which means "little woods" or "little mountain," depending on who you talk to) was in the early portion of the twentieth century. In no way did this adobe qualify as an estate, but still, the ranch was beautiful, so in 1916 it was purchased by a Mr. Cox. He built a polo field near the adobe, renaming it "Ennisbrook." The ranch became a very chic gathering place for wealthy polo enthusiasts, and in 1926 it was sold to Elmer Boeseke, Jr., a polo star who had been on the 1924 gold-medal-winning U.S. Olympic team. Elmer kept up the polo party tradition, and even built stables that would accommodate 150 horses.

*Take a stroll over storybook bridges and through an enchanted forest.*

The glamorous days didn't last forever. The Depression started. In 1936 polo was removed from the Olympics (it's now been reinstated). Then World War II began, and some of the polo stars were killed in action. Boeseke, living in Los Angeles, allowed the ranch to deteriorate, and he passed away in 1965.

Now new owners are enjoying the subdivided estate, but the verdant woods are still available for those of us who can enjoy a mile-and-a-half stroll on flat terrain through an enchanted forest. Spring is the most beautiful time, when nasturtiums, yellow sour-grass, and periwinkle are blooming, but anytime will do. In various stretches, you might imagine that you are one of the first explorers in the area, or that you are in Mexican farming days. It's easy to think about what it was like when the wealthy socialites gathered here in the 1920s. This is a nature walk, but it's also a walk into the past.

**Directions:** From Santa Barbara, go south on Hwy. 101, and exit at San Ysidro Road. Turn left over the freeway. About one block up San Ysidro, turn right on San Leandro Lane. This street turns left, then right; follow the signs. Just past 1710 San Leandro Lane on the left side of the road there is a long white picket fence. If you U-turn, there is room to park in front of this fence. Near the far end of the fence, just past the creek bed, you will see a small path under an oak tree that will take you into Ennisbrook.

**Coastal Cliffways, Goleta.** Most people who know Goleta think of it as predominantly tract housing, research parks, and the home of the University of California at Santa Barbara and the Santa Barbara Airport. Only an occasional resident ventures to the ocean side of UCSB to discover a wild area of plateaus and dunes, beach cliffs and expanses of sand. It's populated by ducks, cranes, and other birds, along with a smattering of humans. To explore this happily under-used area, you may want to park at Goleta Beach if it's a weekday, to avoid UCSB's parking charge. Take Highway 217 off of 101 north, then Sandspit Road toward the airport. At the stop sign, turn left, and the road curves to the beach parking lot.

**Directions:** What follows may be overly detailed, but we want you to get this route right. It's great for walking, but biking will allow you to cover it more easily.

From the Goleta Beach lot, find the bike path heading up the hill toward the campus. At the UCSB entrance above the beach parking lot, turn left on the street and go to the end at the Marine Lab. Behind it is the UCSB Lagoon, surrounded by beaches and dunes. The lagoon is encircled by a dirt path. You can either use this path to get to the low dunes on the opposite side or go up the side of the plateau and along the top. Here, during World War II, Marines practiced their shooting and manned military emplacements, the remains of which can still be found. Quonset huts on campus reflect the time when this area was a Marine base.

At the end of this first plateau, you'll be across the lagoon from the Marine Lab, at some low, flowering ice plant-covered dunes. Go up the side of the second plateau for sweeping sights, or stop and explore the nearly deserted beach here. Follow the second plateau's path heading north and it will go down, then up again at the far end of the lagoon. It leads to Isla Vista, UCSB's student stronghold.

If you go through the post barriers at the end of the dead-end street skirting the ocean here, you'll get a good look at student life, beach-style. It looks casual and carefree, to say the least. Go straight through Isla Vista, which is perhaps a mile long, and at the other end you'll see a path along the ocean. The futuristic condominiums to your right are UCSB faculty-owned.

Beyond the condos, with the ocean cliffs still on your left, you'll pass Devereux, a school for the developmentally disabled. If you veer to the left at the dirt parking area (you need a UCSB permit to park here), you'll find a small building used for seminars by UCSB. This is Coal Oil Point, part of the property once owned by Col. Colin Campbell, a retired English army officer. He and his wife built an elegant two-story estate on what is now Devereux property, where they entertained European royalty during the 1920s. They planted the cypress trees on the point, which is where the Campbells are buried.

Just beyond the seminar building is an entrance to the 157-acre Coal Oil Point Reserve, an ecological study zone managed by UCSB. The reserve is officially closed now to protect the snowy plover nesting sites, but if you are already down on the beach, you are allowed to walk by the reserve area below the high-tide line. A signed nature trail through the dunes is planned for the future, which should be a wonderful educational resource.

If you follow the path to the right from the dirt parking area, you will end up on a road going around the Goleta Slough. The slough is an idyllic, environmentally sensitive area, also used as a study zone by UCSB, and it supports a wide variety of bird life. Near the far end of the slough there's a gradual dirt path going down the hill. The NO TRESPASSING sign refers to the slough area to the left. Go down the path, and you can either follow it all the way around to the wild area at the other side of the slough, or alternatively go up a small rise to connect with the paved track that runs for a short distance along the Ocean Meadows Golf Course.

If you choose the dirt path around the slough, you'll feel like you're on safari. Just obey the signs and stay away from the slough itself. You'll eventually need to reconnect with the paved track before the huge, round-domed storage tanks. On the right, near the storage tanks, the paved track takes you through a metal gate with a pedestrian opening, and ends in another eucalyptus grove. To the north, there's much more in the way of open land and cliffs. Some of it is private property, but much-used by the public especially because the Monarch Point butterfly preserve is in the eucalyptus trees adjacent to this area. It is accessed by car from Hollister Ave. by turning onto Coronado and going to the end.

P.S. If you've ridden your bike as far as the slough, but want a little longer ride before lunch, head toward the mountains to Hollister Avenue and turn left. Follow it to the end for Sandpiper Golf Course's snack shop. The food is nothing special, but their outdoor eating area's view over the golf course and ocean is sublime.

**Carpinteria Seal Sanctuary, Carpinteria Bluffs.** Viewing the seals is just one of the treats to be seen on the bluffs. There are also stately groves of trees, butterflies, birds, broad ocean views, and perhaps paragliders or artists to watch. The Seal Sanctuary bluff area is actually part of Venoco Oil's property, but it has been used for years by the public, and Venoco cooperates. The tidelands down below are state-owned, and the bluffs on the other side of the seal area are now owned by the City of Carpinteria, thanks to major fundraising efforts by Citizens for the Bluffs and assistance from the Land Trust.

This is one of only four areas along the entire Southern California coast where seals bear their young. The animals are protected by the Marine Mammal Protection Act, and during the birthing season from December 1 through May 31 the beach is closed around their habitat. If the seals are disturbed during this time, the adults may abandon the pups. Volunteer "Seal Watchers" are on the bluff to inform the public and make sure no dogs or humans get near the sanctuary. But don't worry, the viewing from above is great.

**Directions:** From the Bailard Avenue exit off Highway 101, turn toward the ocean. There is an area for parking next to the exit, and a wide sandy path leads from there.

Walk through a magnificent meadow, then veer right along a row of eucalyptus trees. At the end of the trees, turn left, cross the railroad tracks, and pick up the trail that bears right. When you near the edge of the bluff, you will see a small area that is marked off by rough cane fencing. In just a five-minute walk through a vintage California landscape, you've reached the Seal Sanctuary, next to the oil pier. Look down on the rocks, and at first you'll think the seals have gone. Look again. They are the same color as the rocks, and there are usually up to one hundred harbor seals in residence. When the tide is out you'll see the most seals because more rocks, which invite lounging, are exposed.

# Art and Antiques

**Rare Books in an 1825 Adobe, 835 Laguna, Santa Barbara, 963-1909**. Ron Randall of Randall House collects and sells fine prints and paintings, rare books and manuscripts. Unlike many rare-book dealers, he doesn't specialize in only one area of interest. Perhaps this is because he's interested in so many things that he can't bear to eliminate entire subjects from his business.

Ron says that "Some of my best friends are five- and ten-dollar books, but I can't afford to stock them. I try to buy only books that sell for over $100, but I don't succeed. Too many less expensive books are fun to read." His shelves are lined with valuable volumes in wonderful old bindings on subjects from western art, history, fishing and hunting to cooking and literature. He figures

*Randall House—an authentic adobe filled with literary treasures.*

that a dozen customers give him maybe fifty percent of his business, as he works with some avid collectors. He puts out a beautiful glossy catalog of his offerings, and quite a few books are sold through the mail and www.randallhouserarebooks.com.

Ron Randall is a lucky man. His store is in one wing of an old adobe that is dripping with Mexican character, and he lives in the other wing. A Señor Gonzalez, who later became alcalde (mayor) of Santa Barbara, built this home. It's been incredibly well preserved. The rooms have vaulted beam ceilings, old brick floors, and almost every room has a fireplace. The exterior doors look ancient, and native desert landscaping completes the picture.

Set above the street and hidden by hedges, you might wonder if you're welcome to enter. Go right ahead, assuming it's business hours. Ron loves to talk about books, art, or the special property he inhabits, and he will even let you peak at his back garden. You really shouldn't miss this Santa Barbara historical treasure.

**Hours:** 9:30 to 5:30 weekdays, 10 to 2 on Saturday.

**Directions:** From State Street, go east on Canon Perdido. Turn right on Laguna and you'll see Randall House's driveway going up the hill on the right. There is parking in the rear.

**For Fervent Photographers, 1321 Alameda Padre Serra, Santa Barbara, 966-3888.** The renowned Brooks Institute trains professional photographers and filmmakers from all over the world at three different campuses in the Santa Barbara area and at their new motion-picture campus in Ventura. The Jefferson campus overlooks the city from a building that originally was a grade school and served as a rehab center for servicemen during World War II. Visitors are welcomed to the photographic gallery that stretches through both levels of hallways, and they can also make onsite use of the library of books and other materials on the art of photography.

Visitors are welcomed to the photographic gallery that stretches the hallways, and they can also make onsite use of the extensive library of books and other materials on the art of photography. In the lower hallway, high quality student work is showcased, while graduate students and faculty display photographs upstairs. You may get to watch students setting up photo shoots in the studios along the halls, and if you're considering applying at the school, there are free comprehensive tours of the Montecito and Jefferson campuses. For those of us with just general interest in the medium, Brooks occasionally gives shows around town when students have produced an important documentary, so ask about those, or check www.brooks.edu.

**Hours:** 8 a.m. to 8 p.m. daily, except when the school is on break.

**Directions:** From State Street, turn on Los Olivos Street toward the mountains. Immediately past the Mission, Alameda Padre Serra ("A.P.S." to locals) veers to the right. The Jefferson Campus is several blocks up on the right.

**Gallery in a Garden, 1040 Mission Canyon Road, Santa Barbara, 682-6724.** Patti Jacquemain has created a little paradise in Mission Canyon, which she calls Mission Creek Studios. A renowned woodcut artist whose work has been shown in a number of cities, Patti has also used her artistic talent to create her home's garden using lush plants, oaks and sycamores, pools and waterfalls. She's even added an additional three acres she calls "Creekspirit," where many of her mosaics have been placed.

Patti is a true Santa Barbaran, having grown up mostly on a ranch near the corner of what is now Alamar and State. She knows the history of Mission Canyon, where she lives, and has been certified a "Master Gardener" by the Botanic Garden just up the road. But her main claim to fame is her woodcut nature print work, which is shown in the gallery at her house, along with her book, *Sweet Seasons.* She occasionally exhibits watercolors and wreaths, and carries blank greeting cards by Santa Barbara artists. People have been known to come up from Los Angeles to buy their Christmas cards here. Being in such a beautiful spot, Mission Creek Studios is a treat to visit, and it's especially nice if Patti is manning the gallery herself. So if your time is flexible, call ahead to find out when she will be there.

**Hours:** Call for appointment; also open November and December weekends 11 a.m. to 4 p.m.

**Directions:** From the Santa Barbara Mission, head toward the mountains on Mission Canyon Road. Turn right on Foothill Road. After about one block, take the ninety-degree curve to the left near the fire station, and the road becomes Mission Canyon Road again. Stay on it when it forks to the right at Tunnel Road. The house is a tall, angular gray stucco building, and is less than one-half mile up from the ninety-degree curve. It's at the far side of a stone bridge on the right side, but go just past the house, turn around, and park in the pull-outs across from her house on the road.

**Santa Barbara's Antique Malls.** Brinkerhoff Avenue is a short street full of historic homes that survived Santa Barbara's devastating 1925 earthquake. Some of them have been converted to antique stores, and one houses the wonderful Peregrine Galleries. It used to be that there wasn't any other real concentration of antique shops in the area, but that was before the advent of the antique mall. Now there are several establishments where many dealers are under one roof, so the dedicated antique shopper can stay very busy in the Santa Barbara area. If you consult the Yellow Pages or the antique guide available at the Visitor Center, you'll find many other single-proprietor shops as well.

*The antique malls in Santa Barbara offer something for everyone.*

- **Antique Alley**, 706 State Street, Santa Barbara, 962-3944. Open 11 a.m. to 6 p.m. Monday through Thursday, until 10 p.m. on Friday and Saturday, and 12 to 5 p.m. on Sunday. About 15 dealers.
- **Goleta Antique Mall**, 5799 Hollister Avenue, Goleta, 967-2528. Open 10 a.m. to 6 p.m., until 5 p.m. on Sunday. Two partners manage this mall of 25 dealers.
- **State Street Antique Mall**, 1219 State Street, Santa Barbara, 965-2575. Open daily from 11 a.m. to 6 p.m., open until 9 p.m. on Fridays and Saturdays. 50 dealers.
- **Summerland Antique Collective**, 2192 Ortega Hill Road, Summerland, 565-3189. Open daily from 10 a.m. to 5 p.m. 35 dealers in two neighboring locations.

**Landscape Paintings in a Landscape Worth Painting, 557 Hot Springs Road, Montecito, 969-5781.** In 1990 a well-known Santa Barbara landscape painter named Marcia Burtt suggested to her friend Ellen Easton that she should open a gallery showing contemporary landscape paintings in her house. Shortly thereafter, Ellen did it, and also rented out a shack in her yard to noted landscape painter Arturo Tello to use as a studio. As luck would have it for Ellen, Arturo and a revered local painter named Ray Strong had recently started an artists' group called the Open Airing Klub, or the OAK Group for short. Through Arturo, Ellen met more landscape artists and eventually came to represent a number of them.

The home is charming, the art is absolutely first class, and Ellen is gracious and welcoming. Her father, Robert Easton, was a famous California writer, and her grandfather, Max Brand, wrote something like 250 western novels. Ellen is carrying on the family literary tradition. She has coordinated and published books on the ranchos surrounding Santa Barbara, the gardens of Santa Barbara, and Ventura County's Santa Clara Valley, all three of which contain historical narrative and showcase paintings done by local landscape artists.

The Easton Gallery may be a little hard to find if you're not familiar with Montecito, but searching it out will give you a chance to see some of this most beautiful area on the way and to visit an old California-style home completely filled with great landscape art when you get there.

**Hours:** 1 p.m. to 5 p.m., Saturday and Sunday only, or by appointment.

**Directions:** From Santa Barbara take 101 south and exit on Olive Mill Road. Turn left. Eventually Olive Mill becomes Hot Springs Road. Turn left on East Valley Road, and right on Parra Grande Lane. Less than a block up you will see an undulating rock wall start on the right side. At the end of this curving wall, there is a gated lane to the right, and 557 Hot Springs Road is the first home on the left inside the gate (Hot Springs Road is reached by following this lane to its other end). There is parking at the house, unless a reception is being held, in which case there will be valet parking.

**Antique Treasures on a Grand Estate, 75 Butterfly Lane, Montecito, 969-1744.** Miraflores, a gorgeous estate near the ocean, was donated to the Music Academy of the West by the secretary of the prior owners after she inherited the property. Here, world-class musicians and singers from all over the world study each summer, and numerous concerts and master classes are open to the public. The Treasure House, located in a small home on the Miraflores grounds, benefits the Academy. Most of the items are there on consignment, with the Academy keeping half the sales price, but some items are donated outright.

Inside, there are several rooms full of well-displayed antique furniture, dishes, paintings, linens, and other collectibles. There is a furniture annex down the hill, where the generally more modern pieces are kept. Because many of Montecito's wealthy moguls are among the Academy's supporters, you never know what riches you may find here. Although prices are not low, dealers often stop by, and the Treasure House's clientele is from a widespread area. Some of them even visit weekly, so as not to miss anything. Income from the operation has increased dramatically in the last few years, generating needed funds and offering consignors an excellent way to sell no-longer-needed, good-quality items. Even if nothing there strikes your fancy, you've at least had the chance to see one of the grand old Montecito estates.

**Hours:** 1 to 4 p.m., Tuesday through Saturday.

**Directions:** From Santa Barbara take 101 south to the left-lane Hot Springs Road exit. Turn right, go under the freeway, and take the first left onto Channel Drive. You will curve right around the cemetery. Turn left on Fairway Road. Just before the "Wrong Way" signs, where the street becomes one way, turn left through the Music Academy entrance at 1070 Fairway. You'll see a small sign pointing down a narrow drive to the left for the Treasure House, but in order to see the mansion, continue on the main tree-lined driveway, turning left when you reach it. You'll go through an archway, then left down an incline. The Treasure House is just to the right at the bottom of the incline. When you exit the property, continue on past the Treasure House, don't double back.

**Peggy's Used Treasures, 4915 Carpinteria Avenue, Carpinteria, 684-2719.** Most family retail businesses with a certain product line have trouble evolving as needs and tastes change. However, Peggy's is one family-owned store that has rolled with the times. It's been an ongoing concern for almost fifty years, but Peggy didn't start out selling collectibles. Pet supplies were her

*You never know what you'll find at Peggy's.*

stock in trade. At that time, horse meat was considered pet food, so that was one of her big sellers.

One day a friend of Peggy's decided to move, and she had 47 small items she wished to sell. Peggy finally consented to display them in her store, and her consignment business was born. Her daughter Dorothy carried on the tradition for many years, although the pet supplies disappeared. She sold the business in 1999 to her employees, gemologist Armando Gonzalez and his wife, Wendy.

There is an assortment of fine things from many Santa Barbara households. The owners have their consignors well trained to know the quality items they'll accept, with their biggest sellers being estate jewelry and sterling silver. Their shelves also showcase china, serving pieces, figurines, glassware and miscellany. If you don't see what you're looking for, give them your name and Wendy will call you when it comes in.

**Hours:** 10 a.m. to 5 p.m. Monday through Saturday.

**Directions:** Going south on 101 from Santa Barbara, exit at Linden Avenue and turn right. Turn right again on Carpinteria Avenue, and you'll see Peggy's ahead on the left.

**Solvang Antique Center, 486 First Street, Solvang, 686-2322.** Entering this second-floor antique collective feels almost like going into a museum. The sixty-five or so dealers here bring in items from across the U.S., and sometimes from Europe. In the 7,000 square feet there are many mantel, wall, and grandfather clocks, antique pianos, paintings, jewelry, furniture, tools, Victrolas, toys, and china. The Center has no similarity to the antique malls of Santa Barbara and Ventura, which carry affordable, sometimes kitschy collectibles. Here, high quality is stressed, and the upper-end price tags indicate that most purchasers would be serious collectors. However, looking is entertaining and free.

**Hours:** 10 a.m. to 6 p.m. daily.

**Directions:** See directions to Sunstone Vineyards, page 41, but turn left off of Highway 246 (Mission Drive) onto First Street, and the Center is one-half block down on the left. If no street parking is available, turn right on Copenhagen Drive and you will see a public lot on the right.

**Art Galleries of Los Olivos, Grand Avenue, Los Olivos.** The history of this delightful little western town is told elsewhere in this book, but art lovers will enjoy Los Olivos as much as history buffs do. Along the two "downtown" blocks of Grand Avenue several art galleries have clustered, along with gift shops and wine-tasting rooms. Don't miss the wonderfully fanciful garden center, J. Woeste, just off the main drag on Alamo Pintado.

As one might expect, western and equestrian arts are featured, but there are many other things to look at, including the artists' collective which shows in Gallery Los Olivos. Be sure to visit the Cody Gallery, which was the first one in town.

The Los Olivos Gallery Organization sponsors several art events during the year. There's a "Ladies First" show in the spring featuring female artists, and a holiday art show on the Saturday after Thanksgiving. Maybe the most fun art event is "Quick Draw" in August, when nationally known artists compete to create the best painting in a 45-minute time period, but you don't need a special-event day to have a good time in Los Olivos.

**Directions:** Take 101 north to the Highway 154/Cachuma Lake exit. Go straight through the light. The road curves. At the next light, turn right onto 154. Go over San Marcos Pass and continue past the turnoff for Highway 246. At Grand Avenue turn left, and note that if you pass Mattei's on 154 you've gone too far. Park somewhere near the flagpole.

**City of Murals, Downtown Lompoc.** The City of Lompoc never had much to recommend to visitors. Its two major attractions, the flower fields and Mission La Purísima, are both outside of town.

But since 1988, local and international artists have been transforming the town into a huge outdoor gallery. There is even a mural done by inmates of the Lompoc Penitentiary as a gift to the city. Along Ocean Avenue and on some side streets, giant murals adorn buildings and suggest the many facets of Lompoc's history. More has gone on there than one might guess, as depicted in murals of Indian villages and the first Spanish mission, the temperance movement, diatomaceous earth mining, steelhead

*The outdoor murals in Lompoc have many stories to tell.*

fishing, ranching, the local flora and fauna, the aerospace industry, and other historic figures and activities.

Most of the murals are permanently displayed, but there is an "Art Alley" between the 100 blocks of South H and I streets, where changing exhibits are located. There is also an area called "Community Canvases" at Chestnut Avenue and North H Street, where works are shown on a rotating basis. Strolling through the murals will take you by a few lovely examples of period architecture as well.

**Directions:** From Santa Barbara take 101 north to Highway 1 toward Lompoc. Turn left on Ocean Avenue/Highway 246. The murals start almost immediately, but the greatest concentration is on and just off Ocean, between E and I streets. A very informative brochure and map of the murals is available weekdays at the Chamber of Commerce, 111 South I Street, 736-4567, or on week-ends between 11:00 and 4:30 p.m. at the Cypress Art Gallery, 119 East Cypress Avenue (from Ocean, turn left on H).

**Antique and Junk Collectors' Dream, East Main Street, Ventura.** Southern California is liberally sprinkled with shiny regional malls selling the new and the trendy. Ventura, meanwhile, has specialized in the old, sometimes quaint, and sometimes simply junky. The largest concentration of stores dealing in second-hand merchandise is on East Main Street, from the 200 through 500 blocks, although you'll find the Goodwill and Easter Seal thrift stores just off Main.

If you browse the area you'll find used and rare books, fine antique furniture, several antique malls stuffed with collectibles (and another good one, Ventura Antique Market, at 457 E. Thompson), military surplus, Bauer pottery, vintage clothing, rummage, and much, much more. Downtown Ventura can be an all-day event if you like to shop for collectibles or bargains. You can grab a great burrito at the taqueria in the 200 block when you need a break, or have a lovely lunch at Nona's Courtyard Cafe in the Bella Maggiore Inn. If you cover it all and still have the stamina for more, the Visitors Bureau at 89-C South California Street has an *Art & Antique Shopping Guide,* which lists shops in other areas of town.

**Hours:** Most stores are open daily, including Sunday. A few are closed one weekday, but there will be plenty to look at any day of the week.

**Directions:** Going south on 101 from Santa Barbara, exit at Main Street, the first offramp for Ventura. Turn right. The 200 block of East Main is just a few blocks up, immediately beyond the Ventura Mission.

**Art City, 1 Peking Street, 648-1690, and 197 Dubbers Street, 653-6380, Ventura.** Ventura's older industrial area is now home to one of the largest suppliers of sculptural quality stone in America. Conceived and run by Paul Lindhard, Art City is a two-location sculpture mecca, where sculptors can get materials, rent studio space, and perhaps show their finished products in Art City's public art garden.

Lindhard used to teach sculpting at Santa Barbara City College, but moved to Ventura in 1984 because he could get a more affordable location here for a sculpture center. The art garden at the corner of Peking and Main streets is being developed, landscaped, and upgraded. In some ways, though, the Dubbers

Street location is the more interesting one, because here one can explore through the areas used by the various artists and maybe see someone at work. Everywhere there are blocks of rock, about a million pounds of it all told, as well as sculptures in progress, tools, rubble, weeds, a blacksmithing area, a huge pile of walnut burls, whimsical metal sculptures, and even a rustic sculpture garden at the back.

Paul is usually at the Dubbers yard, unless he is off on a trip to some exotic place to collect or purchase marble or granite. He buys only rocks that "speak to him" about their sculptural potential, and he must have a good ear. He'll be happy to show sculpture lovers around Art City's Dubbers facility. The place looks chaotic, but it works, and order is slowly emerging.

**Hours:** Wednesday through Sunday, 10 a.m. to 5 p.m.

**Directions:** For Peking Street, from Santa Barbara take Hwy. 101 south and exit at Main Street. Turn right and just over the bridge you'll get to Peking and Main. To reach Dubbers, continue on Main. Turn left on Olive, left on Rex, and right on Dubbers. The two spots are only a few blocks apart.

**The Pottery, 971 McAndrew Road, Ojai, 646-3393.** The Pottery is a combination artist's studio, showroom and home for Otto Heino. He and his wife Vivika have been creating artful pottery for around 50 years, and now that Vivika has passed away, Otto continues their tradition alone. He has received many awards for his work, including a gold medal in a French competition. The Japanese also prize his pieces, and, in fact, one Japanese collector has been coming here every year to purchase approximately $1,000,000 worth of Otto's pottery. This, of course, pleases Otto greatly. "I went right out with the money and bought myself a brand new Rolls Royce, which I'd always wanted," he exclaimed. He'll even show you the car if you're interested.

Heino pottery is known for exquisite glazing and unusual colors, and he has several kilns for different types of firings. After seeing a wood-burning kiln in Japan, Otto installed one at home. It takes twenty hours to stoke up, and Otto has to watch it the whole time. He said, "I can't hire someone to help me. You have to have the rhythm. You have to listen. You can tell by the roar when it needs more wood. It takes a long time, but when you're all done and you open it up, it's like Christmas."

Heino pottery is in museums in Prague and Istanbul, and it's mostly sold to collectors. Prices range from $200 to $25,000. But even if you just wish to come and admire, Otto will welcome you. You'll probably find him in his studio across the breezeway from his showroom. He'll also let you look around his small Japanese garden and koi pond, and his larger garden in back, which he's been working on since he bought the property from his friend and renowned potter, Beatrice Wood.

**Hours:** 1 to 5 p.m., Tuesday through Sunday.

**Directions:** See directions for The Gallery of Historical Figures on page 33. Instead of turning left on McNell, continue out on Reeves Road. McAndrew Road is the next road to the left.

**Hardings: An Antiquarian Delight, 103 West Aliso Street, Ojai, 646-0204.** Hardings is just a couple of blocks off Ojai's main drag, but light years away in terms of content and focus. Here, Englishwoman Lynn Harding operates a fascinating, very specialized business that showcases antique instruments, tools, and even old golf and tennis equipment.

Situated in a quasi-residential neighborhood, the shop is in a charming pitched-roof cottage, but stepping inside is almost like visiting a museum. There are antique scales, globes, microscopes, telescopes, and engineering models of things like oil wells. For the doctor in your life, you can purchase antique surgical sets or other medical equipment. Sailors might like the old nautical instruments, and architects simply must have one of Hardings' antique drafting sets. If Lynn Harding doesn't already have the particular antique instrument you're looking for, she'll find it for you. Although collecting these items is popular in Europe, she is one of very few dealers in the U.S., so a lot of her business is done through mail order. She welcomes visitors, though, and has items starting at about the $100 level. The looking is free.

**Hours:** Noon to 5 p.m., Friday through Monday, or by appointment.

**Directions:** Coming into Ojai on Highway 150 from Santa Barbara, turn left on North Ventura Street (the library is on the corner; if you get to the arched Arcade you've gone too far). Aliso Street is two blocks up. Turn left and you'll see Hardings.

**Wildling Art Museum, 2329 Jonata Street, Los Olivos, 688-1082.** A "wildling" is a wild plant, bird, or animal, and this miniature museum in a historic home is dedicated to promoting appreciation of America's wilderness. They are establishing a small but choice art collection of their own, but their revolving exhibits also showcase paintings, prints, sculpture and photography on loan from major art museums. The Wildling is just a short stroll from Los Olivos' galleries and wine tasting rooms, and they have a garden in the works to enjoy, too.

**Hours:** Wednesday through Friday 1 to 5 p.m., week-ends 11 a.m. to 5 p.m.

**Directions:** See page 73 for Los Olivos. At the flagpole, turn right on Alamo Pintado, then right on Nojoqui. The museum is just past St. Mark's Episcopal Church, and just before you reach the famous Mattei's Tavern, which faces Hwy. 154.

*The Wildling's idyllic location combines wilderness art with Old West surroundings.*

# Uncommon Merchants and Manufacturers' Outlets

**Santa Barbara's Ethnic Markets.** For a town with a reputation for harboring the rich and famous, and having the chic delis and food shops that cater to them, the Santa Barbara area also has quite a collection of decidedly untrendy ethnic food stores. Large numbers of English, Germans, Italians, Mexicans, Vietnamese and other nationalities have settled in "America's Riviera," and many of them have opened authentic markets catering to their own culinary tastes. Here is a list of them, just in case you're an exotic food junky like me. The Asian markets are located in Goleta, where these nationalities have tended to settle.

- **Italian Grocery**, 415 E. De la Guerra, 966-6041. Italian deli, wines, foodstuffs.
- **The Italian and Greek Delicatessen**, 636 State, 962-6815.
- **Oriental Market**, 420 South Fairview in the Airport Plaza, 683-4417. Vietnamese, Thai, some Indian condiments.
- **Choi's Oriental Market**, 185 S. Patterson in the Patterson Center, 683-1892. Chinese and other Asian foods.
- **Indo-China Market**, 6831 Hollister in the K-Mart Center, 968-3353.
- **Nikka Oriental Groceries**, 5721 Calle Real, 964-7396. Japanese.
- **Chapala Market**, 605 North Milpas, 963-2039. Great selection of Mexican foods.

**Magellan's, 110 West Sola Street, Santa Barbara, 568-5400 or 1-800-962-4943.** This Santa Barbara-based company claims to be the leading source of travel products. Ninety-five percent of their business is mail order through their quarterly catalog, but you can also visit their showroom. They carry over six hundred items, and should be able to help you with just about any travel gear need.

**Hours:** 9 a.m. to 5:30 p.m., Monday through Saturday.

**Directions:** Heading up State Street (going away from the ocean), turn left on Sola, and the store is one and a half blocks up Sola on the right side.

**Jordano's Marketplace, 3025 De La Vina Street, Santa Barbara, 965-3031.** If you are a serious cook or just love to set a pretty table, this is the place for you. Jordano's has a huge selection of gadgets, pots and pans, dishes, gourmet food and wine, cookbooks, and appliances from blenders to restaurant-quality ovens. Jordano's has plenty of experience knowing what is needed in the kitchen. The four Jordano brothers opened a grocery in 1915, and now the company consists of a large beer and wine distributorship, a food-service division that supplies many commercial operations (including the oil rigs off the coast), and the Marketplace. Jordano's is not a discount store. It is special because of the depth of its merchandise, and amateur chefs could spend quite a while here.

**Hours:** 9 a.m. to 7 p.m. Monday through Saturday, Sunday 10 a.m. to 6 p.m.

**Directions:** De La Vina is parallel to State Street, two blocks west. Because it is one-way going toward the ocean for over two miles, take State up to Calle Laureles, turn left, then right on De La Vina, and Jordano's will be just ahead on your left.

**Territory Ahead, 400 State Street, Santa Barbara, 962-5558.** This Santa Barbara success story has grown into a national mail-order company, selling quality casual wear for men and women. Their only retail store is at 515 State, but the bargains are at their outlet at 400 State, where discontinued clothing is sold for 30-40 percent off. If there's something you like, you'll be getting sturdy clothing at a good price.

**Hours:** 10 a.m. to 6 p.m. Monday through Saturday, 11 a.m. to 5 p.m. Sunday.

**Directions:** The outlet is at the corner of Gutierrez and State, about a block from the retail store.

**Pacific Co., 3309A State Street, Santa Barbara, 682-9552.** Santa Barbara's long standing houseplant and import store, Pacific Co.'s wares have gotten more "diverse" as the years have gone by. Some might say their buyer has run amok. Next to the baskets, plants and potting supplies are party paper goods, greeting cards, lipstick, candy, and seasonal kitsch. For the kids, costume items and hundreds of novelties like finger puppets and rubber frogs are displayed. There's miniature furniture and figurines, a shell collection, and inexpensive area rugs. In other words, Pacific Co. has something for everyone.

**Hours:** 10 a.m. to 6 p.m. Monday through Friday, til 5 p.m. on Saturday, 12 to 4 p.m. on Sunday.

**Directions:** Going up State Street, pass the Las Positas intersection, and turn left into the Loreto Plaza parking lot. Pacific Co. is next to the Wherehouse.

**Santa Barbara Ceramic Design, 436 East Gutierrez Street, Santa Barbara, 966-3883 x122.** A local manufacturer since 1976, Ceramic Design's products used to be handpainted by employees working at home. Now they have a large manufacturing facility in Santa Barbara, and everything is silkscreened. Their dishes, plaques, clocks, and trivets are carried by 8,000 retailers in the U.S. and Canada. Discounted seconds are sold here at their onsite factory outlet, and other potters' products are priced at retail. This company is a major Santa Barbara success.

**Hours:** 10 a.m. to 5 p.m. daily.

**Directions:** Gutierrez is one way, heading towards State Street. So if you're coming from downtown, go down Anacapa Street, turn left on Haley Street, and right on Olive. The outlet's entrance is actually on Olive, near the corner of Gutierrez.

**Jedlicka's Saddlery, 2605 De La Vina Street, Santa Barbara, 687-0747.** Santa Barbara is, after all, in the West, and Jedlicka's is the quintessential western purveyor. It's one of the longest standing businesses in town, and the Jenkins family has been involved with this store since 1946. They've been entwined with the West a bit longer, as their ancestors came to California during the Gold Rush.

The Jenkins clan has always been active in the area's equestrian scene. Father Si was on the Board of the local Showgrounds for many years, and son Josiah, now Jedlicka's manager, is a past chairman of the Fiesta Stock Horse Show and Rodeo. They are also members of other equestrian organizations, and they know what horse owners need. Their 8,000 square foot store is chockablock with western and English riding togs, cowboy hats and boots, and horse tack and gear for roping and for trail, hunt and show riding. For those who only like horses at a distance, there's plenty of western wear and silver jewelry to make Jedlicka's a fun stop.

**Hours:** 9:00 a.m. to 5:30 p.m., Monday through Saturday.

**Directions:** From downtown, go up State Street through a residential area, and turn left on Constance Avenue. De La Vina is two blocks down, parallel to State, and Jedlicka's is near the corner. You can usually park on Constance.

**Deckers Outdoor Corp. Factory Outlet Store, 4880 Colt Street, Ventura, 676-3571.** Two college hippy surfers started making leather thong sandals in their garage in the early '70's. Before they knew it, they had perhaps 80 employees and a booming business selling Deckers, the layered rubber beach thongs. The business has gone through many stages, but today Deckers is a public corporation, and one of the original two guys still runs the show. The company controls Teva sport sandals, UGG Boots, and Simple shoes. Their only outlet has a big supply of discontinued and "distressed" pairs of footwear, and Teva's wonderfully comfortable outdoor clothing at cheap prices. They call it, "Parking lot sale prices everyday!"

By the way, you don't need to worry about the other original partner. He's doing just fine as C.E.O. of QAD Software in Carpinteria, one of the largest manufacturing software companies in the world.

**Hours:** Monday through Friday 12 to 6 p.m., Saturday 10 a.m. to 6 p.m., Sunday 11 a.m. to 5 p.m.

**Directions:** Going south on 101 from Santa Barbara, exit at Telephone Road in Ventura, and turn left onto Main Street. At Main's intersection with Telephone, jog right onto Valentine, which parallels the freeway. Turn right on Palma, then left on Colt.

**Arte D'Italia Imports, 19 Helena, Santa Barbara, 564-7655.** The Parrucca Collection of handmade, vividly colored pottery from Palermo is featured here, with most pieces depicting aspects of life in Sicily. There are other items such as Murano glassware, frames, bath items, and a couple other lines of Italian pottery. Arte D'Italia is the sole U.S. representative for Parrucca, who studied art under a follower of Picasso's, and this training is evi-

dent in his work. Prices here are around 75 percent of retail, and range from $6 to $1,000.

**Hours:** 10 a.m. to 6 p.m. daily, closing at 5 p.m. in winter.

**Directions:** Helena is a one-block long street between State and Anacapa, running into Cabrillo Boulevard on Santa Barbara's beachfront. This is a fun area to poke around, as there are many other shops and sights within walking distance, so park where you are allowed to stay for awhile.

**Big Dog Sportswear, 6 East Yanonali Street, Santa Barbara, 963-8727.** Big dogs are all over this line of high-quality, reasonably priced clothing for men, women, and children. At their hometown outlet next to the corporate offices, there are substantial discounts on test garments, overruns, and samples, as well as their regular retail merchandise. The clothing exemplifies the Southern California lifestyle, and in fact, shots of Santa Barbara are shown throughout their catalog. In bankruptcy in 1992, the company made a dramatic comeback under new management. They've gone from four stores to a hundred, added mail order, and are now targeting the European market.

Where did the name come from? A group on a river-rafting trip in 1983 were given pairs of brightly colored, oversized shorts. Everyone loved them, and they all kept saying, "Man, these puppies are BIG!"

**Hours:** 10 a.m. to 6 p.m. Sunday through Thursday, until 7 p.m. Friday and Saturday.

**Directions:** Big Dogs is actually on State Street, on the ocean side of 101.

**Island View, 3376 Foothill Road, Carpinteria, 684-0324.** Hidden away near the Carpinteria Polo Club and Stewart Orchids is a business that calls itself a nursery, but is really much more. Island View's front area consists of garden vignettes with an asian influence, showcasing pots, benches, statuary, ornaments, plants and rocks. But the big surprise is inside.

Owner Windy Overbach was vacationing in Bali, and just couldn't resist going shopping. A year later, he has a 12,000-

square-foot showroom of imported antiques and other furnishings, plus decorative items, jewelry and even food items from places like China, Indonesia, Bali and Zimbabwe. So far, though, they are resisting marketing these treasures over the internet as Windy really wants Island View to be a resource for Santa Barbara area locals.

At the rear of the ten-acre property is their 100,000-square-foot greenhouse complex, specializing in plants such as specimen palms, dracaenas, and orchids. The public is welcome to stroll the aisles and pick from among this huge array, although how do you choose from a selection this large?

**Hours:** 9 a.m. to 5 p.m. daily, however, Sundays are seasonal.

**Directions:** Going south on 101 from Santa Barbara, exit at Padaro Lane. Turn left over the freeway, then right on Via Real. At the end of the polo field, turn left on Nidever, which becomes Foothill. The entrance is across the road from the Polo and Racquet Club condo entrance.

**Art From Scrap, 302 East Cota Street, 884-0459.** Entering this warehouse-like building, anyone who likes to do crafts or make collages will probably feel overwhelmed and overjoyed.

*At Art From Scrap, look in the bottom of every barrel.*

Barrel upon barrel of recycled materials of all sorts are there to be purchased at $7 per bagfull, and many other items are priced. A few of the things available are neoprene cutouts, cardboard tubes, long curly plastic shavings which are created in the manufacture of skateboard wheels, plastic confetti, beads, buttons, old eyeglasses, fabric, colored sand, special sticks, test tubes, and little toy animals. There are also immediately useable items, such as junk jewelry, pretty computer stationery sold by weight, greeting cards and wrapping paper, but all this is just the beginning. You'll have to see for yourself, and the supply changes all the time.

Art From Scrap is operated by the nonprofit Community Environmental Council, and all supplies are donated by industrial companies, individuals, and craft stores. They welcome school field trips, when the students learn about recycling and get to make something. AFS also hosts birthday parties in the art studio, as well as scheduled art workshops. In their store, they display examples of wonderfully creative and whimsical art pieces that have been made with their materials, so get your imagination in gear and go.

**Hours**: Tuesday, Wednesday and Friday 10 a.m. to 2 p.m., Thursday 10 a.m. to 6 p.m., Saturday 10 a.m. to 3 p.m.

**Directions:** Art From Scrap is at the corner of Garden and Cota Streets, just three blocks from State Street's Old Town.

**The Rack, 73 Butterfly Lane, Montecito, 969-0190.** The Rack is located in Miraflores, the gorgeous estate that now houses the Music Academy of the West, along with the Treasure House antique shop. After driving through the grounds, visitors walk by a charming sunken patio before entering the Rack's Mediterranean-style house. The previously owned clothes sold by The Rack are all donated outright to support the Academy, and you never know when you may find a designer bargain that has been worn only once or twice.

**Hours:** 1 to 4 p.m. Tuesday through Saturday.

**Directions:** The Rack is next door to the Treasure House (see page 71).

**Pacific Travellers Supply, 12 West Anapamu St., 963-4438.** Originally from Germany, Jan Koch was an airline employee assigned to look for new ways to market the airline. He saw that travel stores might serve that function, but he also saw an opportunity for himself. So he left the airline, and today owns four travel stores. He took a gamble and purchased Pacific Travellers Supply after 9/11, when travel activity slowed way down. He's hoping his store's policy of free shipping anywhere in the U.S., liberal exchange policy and $5 credit for each $35 spent, along with renewed interest in travel will make his newest store a success. It's a good place to go for luggage, guidebooks, maps, travel accessories and clothing.

**Hours:** 10 a.m. to 8 p.m. daily, except winter Sundays closing at 6 p.m.

**Directions:** Going up State Street, turn left on Anapamu Street (walking only, cars can't turn left) and the store will be on your right.

**Teddy Bears Factory Outlet, 4185-1 Carpinteria Avenue, Carpinteria, 566-4883.** In an industrial building just off the 101 freeway, these whimsical merchants are offering sixty different manufacturer's bears, bunnies, dogs, and other creatures for sale at the lowest prices allowed by their makers. Prices are actually monitored in person by some of the manufacturers reps to make sure nothing is going too cheap, but compared to retail shops you can still get good savings on Steiff, Gund, Merry Thought, and others, as well as animals made by artists who are featured in magazines like *Teddy Bear Review.*

**Hours:** 10 a.m. to 4 p.m. Monday through Saturday. Closed Tuesday.

**Directions:** Going south on 101 from Santa Barbara, exit at Carpinteria Avenue. The bears are in the first building on the right as you exit.

**Eye of the Day, 4620 Carpinteria Avenue, Carpinteria, 566-0778.** This store, selling garden decor pieces including pots galore, fountains, statuary and upscale garden ornaments, was a popular purveyor near Solvang, but in 1998 they were flood victims of El Niño. They had already made plans for a second store in Carpinteria, but the flood led them to concentrate on this alternative location, which has fluorished.

The store's name has a double entendre, by the way. The owners' daughter is named Daisy. The owner explained that "day's eye" in old English meant the sun, and in a convoluted way, they wanted to name their garden center after their daughter.

**Hours:** Daylight Savings hours 9 a.m. to 6 p.m. Wednesday through Saturday, 10 a.m. to 5 p.m. Sunday and Monday. Winter hours 9 a.m. to 5 p.m. Wednesday through Saturday.

**Directions:** Going south on 101 from Santa Barbara, exit at Carpinteria Avenue. Not far past Santa Ynez Avenue, you'll see Eye of the Day, which shares a driveway with a Coco's restaurant.

**Bart's Corner, 302 W. Matilija, Ojai, 666-3755.** This bookstore is the ultimate in "country casual." There is no roof, and some of the books are displayed outside the store's entrance, so they are always accessible. A sign asks that you drop your money through the door slot when they are closed.

A Mr. Bartindale used to own this circa-1935 house, and he

*Readers love Bart's Corner.*

started building outdoor bookshelves in 1964. Gary Schlichter took over in 1976 and, like Mr. Bartindale, he lives on the property. He offers more than 100,000 used volumes for sale now, which are organized by subject in alcoves, and there are tables and chairs available for browsers. Book lovers often develop quite an affection for Bart's, and one couple even got married there.

**Hours:** 10 a.m. to 5:30 p.m. Tuesday to Sunday.

**Directions:** When entering Ojai on 150, turn left on Canada Street (before you get to the downtown Arcade). Bart's is one block up at the corner of Canada and Matilija.

# Sports City

The Santa Barbara area offers a huge array of outdoor sporting activities, due to its mountainous topography and its proximity to the ocean. To access the many hiking trails, consult one of the excellent trail guides which are carried by the Santa Barbara Visitor Center and the local bookstores. If you wish to play tennis, Santa Barbara's public courts may be used by anyone, with payment of a small daily fee. Here are other activities you can consider, and the operators to contact. Listings are in the Santa Barbara area unless noted otherwise.

## ◆ *On the Water*

**Channel Islands Excursions**

- Truth Aquatics, one and multi-day trips, camping or live-aboard, 962-1127.
- Island Packers in Ventura Harbor, one or multiple day trips to the islands, recorded information 642-7688, reservations 642-1393 .

**Deep Sea Fishing**

- Sea Landing, 963-3564. Half to full day fishing trips.

**Diving**

- Truth Aquatics, 962-1127. One, two and three day dive boat trips. Equipment rentals available.
- Anacapa Dive Center, dive classes, 963-8917.

**Jet Boat rentals**

- Sea Landing, 963-3564. Wave runners and four person jet boat rentals.
- Santa Barbara Sailing Center, 962-2826. Power boat rentals.

**Kayaking**

- Paddle Sports, 899-4925. Kayak rentals at Santa Barbara Harbor. Lessons, coastal kayak trips, and 1-2 day island trips.
- Adventours Outdoor Excursions, 899-2929. Kayak trips to the Channel Islands, April through November.

**Sailboat rentals and cruises**

- Santa Barbara Boat Rentals, 962-2826. 16'-42' keel boats and charter yachts, bare boat (with experience) or skippered. Cruises on the Double Dolphin catamaran, including sunset champagne, jazz or dinner cruises, and afternoon coastal cruises.

**Surfing**

- The Beach House, 963-1281. Doyle surfboards, boogie boards and wetsuits for rent.

**Whale Watching**

- Sea Landing, 963-3564. 75-foot *Condor Express,* trips accompanied by Whale Corps members from the Marine Sanctuary.

**Wildlife Cruises**

- Lake Cachuma in the Santa Ynez Valley, reservations 568-2460. Two hour eagle cruises November-February, wildlife cruises March-October, $12 for adults, $5 kids under 6.

## ◆ *Up in the Air*

**Glider Rides**

- Windhaven Glider Rides at the Santa Ynez Airport, 688-2517.
- Sky Dive Santa Barbara, 740-9099. Tandem jumps and accelerated free-fall courses, based at Lompoc Airport.

**Paragliding Lessons**

- Fly Above All, 965-3733. Paragliding is the easy-to-learn successor to hang gliding. You will have solo flights during your first lesson at the training hill.

**Parasailing**

- Blue Edge Para-Sailing, 966-5206. Boat-towed parasailing with dry take-offs and landings. No experience necessary.

**Sightseeing Plane Rides**

- Santa Paula Airport, first Sunday of each month, 933-1155.

## ◆ *Land-based Locomotion*

**Bicycle, Mountain Bike, Surrey, and Rollerblade rentals**

- Cycles 4 Rent, 101 State Street, 340-BIKE or 1-888-405-BIKE. Also at the Doubletree and Radisson Hotels, Lake Casitas and the Ventura bike path.
- Beach Rentals, 22 State Street, 966-6733.

**Guided Bike Rides**

- Pedal & Paddle (Judy Keim), 687-2912. Custom bike tours, including special interest routes for bird watching, outdoor art, etc.

**Golf (Public)**

- Santa Barbara Golf Club, 687-7087, 18 hole course.
- Twin Lakes Golf Course, Goleta, 964-1414, 9 hole 3-par course.
- Ocean Meadows Golf Course, Goleta, 9 hole course.
- Glen Annie Golf Club, Goleta, 968-6400, 18 hole championship course, nice restaurant.
- Sandpiper Golf Course, Goleta, 968-1541, spectacular ocean-side 18 hole course.
- Rancho San Marcos Golf Course, Santa Ynez Valley, 683-6334, scenic 18 hole course.

*The bikepath along Santa Barbara's beachfront is a magnet for bicyclists, runners, walkers, and skaters.*

**Horseback Riding**

- Arriba Horse Adventures, 551-8567. Small group rides on the ocean bluffs and onto the beach in Goleta. One day's advance reservation preferable.
- Circle Bar B Stables, Refugio Road (45 minutes from Santa Barbara), 968-3901. 90 minute scenic walking rides up into the mountains near President Reagan's former ranch.
- Rancho Oso Stables, Paradise Road (approximately 35 minutes from Santa Barbara in the Santa Ynez Mountains), 683-5110. One hour walking-only rides.

**Kite Flying**

- Come Fly a Kite, 1228 State Street, 966-2694. Great kite selection for sale 7 days a week. Favorite Santa Barbara spots for kite flying are Shoreline Park and Mission Meadow (across the street from the Mission).

## Other Entertainments

Besides the sporting activities above and the "secrets and side-trips" in this book, there are plenty of other things to do in the Santa Barbara area. Check *The Independent,* Santa Barbara's free weekly newspaper, for up-to-date listings of special events, plays, concerts, and art openings. Here are a few other ideas:

**Bookstore Programs:** Most of Santa Barbara's bookstores offer occasional book signings, talks by authors, and music or children's programs. However, a few stores are especially active:

- **Borders Books & Music, 900 State Street, 899-3668.** Frequent lectures and musical events.
- **Chaucer's Books, 3321 State Street, 682-6787.** Saturday children's storytime, famous author book signings.
- **Sullivan Goss Books & Prints, 7 East Anapamu Street, 730-1460.** Fine art shows, art receptions, and musical dinner shows.

**Casino Gambling:** After more than one contract operator failed, the Chumash Indians have now made a big success of their casino on Highway 246 in Santa Ynez. They're the biggest employer in the Santa Ynez Valley, and the profits have improved their standard of living immensely. There's a 1,200-seat bingo pavilion, restaurant, video games, a separate poker room, and an area for "Chumash 21." Card players can call 686-0855 two hours ahead of arrival to get on the play list. Free bingo buses, and occasional big-name entertainment. 1-800-728-9997 for information. Open 24 hours Wednesday through Saturday, 10 a.m. to 2 a.m. Sunday through Tuesday. No children under 18 admitted.

**Day Spa Services:** Get a facial or a massage. Consult the Yellow Pages for the practitioner most convenient to you.

**Horse Racing:** Wagering at Earl Warren Showgrounds, Las Positas Road at Highway 101. Races shown live via satellite from all of California's tracks. 687-0766 for track info and post times.

# Night Life

Santa Barbara is an extremely active town culturally, with over a dozen theatre groups, and a number of venues for concerts and other types of shows. These shows will be listed in The Independent weekly newspaper. Nightclubs for those under twenty-five are easy to find, as many of them are clustered in and near the 400 to 600 blocks of State Street. For those who are slightly more mature, and want to hear some music and perhaps dance in a little less frenetic environment, the venues are not as obvious. Here are some places in Santa Barbara to check.

**Andria's,** 214 State Street, 966-3000. Thursday jazz, Friday and Saturday pop, occasional entertainment other nights.

**Bistro 1111,** 1111 E. Cabrillo Blvd. in the Radisson Hotel, 730-1111. Jazz or piano bar from 9:30 p.m. on Friday and Saturday nights. Dance floor.

**Carrillo Recreation Center,** 100 E. Carrillo St., 965-3813. Swing dancing first and third Fridays of each month, 8:30 to midnight, $10. Ballroom dancing every Saturday night from 8 to 11 p.m., $9, or $14 including 7 p.m. lesson. Huge spring-loaded floor, not much atmosphere, but great for dancing enthusiasts.

**Cold Spring Tavern,** 5995 Stagecoach Road (see page 27), 967-0066. Live blues, bluegrass or rock on Friday nights, Saturday and Sunday afternoons. Very popular with motorcyclists.

**Dargan's,** 18 East Ortega Street, 568-0702. Traditional Irish group plays Thursdays starting at 5:30 p.m.

**The James Joyce,** 513 State Street, 962-2688. Jazz on Saturday afternoons and evenings, as well as Sunday afternoon.

**Four Seasons Biltmore Hotel,** 1260 Channel Dr., Montecito, 969-2261. Entertainment Tuesday through Saturday from 7:30 p.m. in La Sala Lounge. Music offered ranges from solo piano to swing or jazz. Small dance floor, call for schedule.

**Rocks,** 801 State Street, 884-8485. Frequent live rock and jazz, dancing, young stylish crowd, call for schedule.

**Plow and Angel,** 900 San Ysidro Ln. at San Ysidro Ranch, Montecito, 969-5046. Historic and charming cellar bar at this luxury resort ranch features jazz on Friday and Saturday nights from 9:00 to midnight.

**Soho,** 1221 State St., 962-7776. Second floor restaurant and music club with high ceilings, red brick walls and outdoor deck. Music every night, including jazz, blues, reggae, folk, acoustic and world music, and dancing when appropriate. Entertainment starts at 7:30 or 8:00 p.m. on weeknights, and 9:30 p.m. on week-ends, also mellow jazz during dinner on week-ends.

# Bed and Breakfast Inns

**Bath Street Inn, 1720 Bath Street, Santa Barbara, 682-9680, or 1-800-549-BATH in Ca., 1-800-341-BATH in U.S.** The Bath Street Inn was one of Santa Barbara's first B&B's when it opened in 1981, and the 1890's Queen Anne Victorian is still a welcoming sight to its guests. The owner calls it "Carpenter's Gothic," in other words, the carpenter did whatever he pleased. The owner's style is casual, and her inn isn't as formal as some others. The rooms are furnished nicely, but please note that there is no real garden, just a patio, and it is situated a few blocks farther from downtown and the beach than most other inns. It is, however, the closest B&B to Sansum Clinic and Cottage Hospital.

**Rooms with Private Bath:** 12.

**Amenities Available:** Jacuzzi tubs, fireplaces, VCR's. Televisions and phones in all rooms. Refrigerator and TV/VCR in public area upstairs.

**Nearby:** Downtown 7 blocks.

**Price Range:** $85-$240.

**The Bayberry Inn, 111 West Valerio Street, Santa Barbara, 569-3398.** The Bayberry Inn is quite a family operation. Owners Kenneth and Jill Freeland live a couple of blocks away, but their aunt and uncle live at the property and work respectively as Innkeeper and Chef. All four are actively involved, and have upgraded the gardens and rooms since buying the inn a couple of years ago.

A rococo, opulent decorating style is present, which was originally instituted by former male proprietors with an interior design background. The rooms have dramatic canopy beds and rich

color schemes. There is a spacious dining room and a lovely garden and deck, where guests eat their full cooked breakfast between 9:00 and 10:00. Coffee and tea are always available, and they serve wine and cheese from 4:00 to 6:00, and cookies for an evening treat.

**Rooms with Private Bath:** 9.

**Amenities Available:** Jacuzzi tubs, private terraces, fireplaces, televisions.

**Nearby:** Downtown 4 blocks.

**Price Range:** $99-$229.

**Blue Dolphin Inn, 420 West Montecito Street, Santa Barbara, 965-2333.** This inn's location has some definite pluses and minuses. On the positive side, it's right next door to the historic home called Fernald House (open the first Sunday of each month from 2 to 4 p.m.), and the harbor and beach are within walking distance. Less attractively, the inn sits on a very busy street, near motels and convenience stores, and it does not have a garden. However, if you don't care about strolling around the yard or the neighborhood you are residing in, you'll enjoy the Blue Dolphin.

Formerly called the Harbour Carriage House, this Victorian bungalow was rehabilitated, and a new "carriage house" was added in the rear. The rooms are furnished with antiques and wicker, along with some upholstery personally done by the former Moroccan-French proprietess. The Blue Dolphin's owners are now Peter and Ed, who both have a hospitality industry background. Pete, a Santa Barbara native, attended Santa Barbara City College's highly regarded hotel and restaurant management program, while Ed formerly owned a B&B and a restaurant in Chicago.

Their two least expensive rooms are entered directly from the living room, so the feeling of privacy isn't as great as the other rooms. Upstairs, there is one large loft room which can accommodate a family of four, complete with toys for the kids. The other room is small but cozy and has large windows framed by trees, giving one the feeling of being in a treehouse looking down on Fernald House. In the carriage house rooms more amenities are available, but the less expensive rooms offer the same level of charm. As for food, breakfast is served from 8 to 10 a.m. in the solarium, and there's wine and cheese in the afternoon.

**Rooms with Private Baths:** 9.

**Amenities Available:** Fireplaces, jacuzzi tubs, balconies, TV's with VCR (videos available). Phone in all rooms, handicap access.

**Nearby:** Public tennis courts one block, ocean two blocks, downtown 7 blocks.

**Price Range:** $98-$245.

**Casa Del Mar, 18 Bath Street, Santa Barbara, 963-4418, 1-800-433-3097** for reservations. Yun and Yessy Kim's property which was developed in 1927 as beach bungalows and two Spanish-style houses, which were blended to create a 21 unit inn. The Casa has Mediterranean charm and a little quirkiness, because of the historic nature of the property. The buildings surround a central courtyard with outdoor jacuzzi, and the staff is pleasant. There are one and two room suites available, and many guests will appreciate the comforts of having a sitting area or living room. They will even accept some pets, with a $10 per night additional charge, and unlike other bed and breakfast inns, they allow children.

An expanded continental breakfast is served from 7:30 to 10:00 a.m., and they offer wine and cheese from 5:00 to 7:00 p.m. This inn is not a fussy B&B, and for those who enjoy something a little different, and want a fairly central location near the ocean, this may be a good choice.

**Rooms or Suites with Private Bath:** 21.

**Amenities Available:** Balconies, kitchens, kitchenettes, fireplaces. TV and phone in all rooms.

**Nearby:** Restaurants, ocean and bike path 1/2 block, yacht harbor 2 blocks, downtown 7 blocks.

**Price Range:** $89-$279.

**Cheshire Cat Inn, 36 West Valerio Street, Santa Barbara, 569-1610.** The Cheshire Cat's owner revived side by side stately but dilapidated homes to produce this inn. Nice architectural details include beautiful plank flooring and high ceilings. Guests can order their breakfast to be delivered to their rooms between 8:30 and 10:00, or they can eat outside on the cozy brick patio, or in the dining room. Also in the garden is a lovely, large gazebo with a jacuzzi, and a shaded deck for relaxing. For the more ambitious, there are two bicycles for guests' use.

The theme here, as one might guess from the inn's name, is Alice in Wonderland, although it's not overdone. Rooms have names like "The White Rabbit," and the decor includes English antiques, brass beds and Laura Ashley wallpapers. It's all accomplished very professionally, and is quite luxurious.

**Rooms with Private Bath:** 21.

**Amenities Available:** Jacuzzi tubs, fireplaces, private deck, refrigerators, telephones, televisions. Two bedroom cottages have full kitchens and private hot tubs.

**Nearby:** Downtown 4 blocks.

**Price Range:** $150-$375.

**Country Inn By the Sea, 128 Castillo Street, Santa Barbara, 963-4471, 1-800-455-4647.** Originally a three-story motel, this inn was utterly and completely refurbished in 1995. The owners have done everything humanly possible to turn an architecturally uninteresting box into an inviting, well-decorated and charming inn, and they've succeeded. Outside there are beautiful plantings, and vines entwined around all the railings. Inside, wonderful wallpapers and fabrics, along with pine accents, have been combined to create a very appealing decor. Even Elmer Dills, the *Los Angeles Times* food and travel columnist, thinks so, as he is a repeat guest here.

An expanded continental breakfast is served in the luxurious lobby from 7:30 to 11:00 a.m., and every afternoon the staff bakes cookies. This staff, by the way, seems especially friendly and efficient, and they keep the place immaculate. The Country Inn is a great combination of hotel and bed and breakfast, in that you have amenities like a pool, outdoor jacuzzi, sauna, air conditioning, and ice machines, which most bed and breakfasts don't have, and you get breakfast and B&B charm thrown in.

**Rooms with Private Bath:** 45. Some are quite large.

**Amenities Available:** Jacuzzi tubs, balconies, VCR's. Videotape and book libraries for guests to use. TV, phone and small refrigerator in all rooms. Elevator.

**Nearby:** Public tennis courts in the park across the street, ocean one block, downtown 7 blocks.

**Price Range:** $109-$219.

**Glenborough Inn, 1327 Bath Street, Santa Barbara, 966-0589, 1-800-962-0589.** The Glenborough's original owner went on to head a national bed and breakfast association. Now Marlies Marburg, a German woman, owns it, and has expanded the operation to five homes on the same block. They offer a variety of rooms and prices, some with private entrances. Facilities including the parlor, hot tub and garden at the 1906 Craftsman main house are shared by all the guests.

Wine and hors d'oeuvres are served in the late afternoon on Fridays and Saturdays, while a hot breakfast is delivered to the

*Rose fanciers will appreciate the Glenborough's garden.*

rooms between 8:00 and 9:30. This arrangement may especially appeal to those who want privacy yet enjoy a B&B-style ambience.

**Rooms with Private Baths:** 16.

**Amenities Available:** Private outdoor hot tub, private patio, fireplaces, coffee makers, some tv/vcr's, robes.

**Nearby:** 3 blocks to downtown, 4 to Art Museum, 1 mile to beach.

**Price Range:** $120-$300.

**Inn of the Spanish Garden, 915 State Street, 564-4700, 1-866-564-4700.** Newly constructed in 2001 at the edge of downtown, this inn is actually a small hotel, as opposed to a B&B. But they do include an expanded continental breakfast with quiche or fritatta, served from 7:30 on in your room or the dining room. They also have a fine local wine collection, and do tastings in the evening.

There is a lovely Spanish-style courtyard, and almost every amenity you can think of has been provided. If you are looking for a small luxury inn with tasteful decor, located very conveniently to downtown and with all the amenities, the Inn of the Spanish Garden is perfect.

*Inn of the Spanish Garden*

**Rooms with Private Baths:** 23 (6 are suites).

**Amenities Available:** Covered parking, lap pool, wedding garden, conference rooms, high-speed internet access, fitness machines, balconies or private gardens, french press coffee makers, minibars, oversize soaking tubs, robes, newspaper, concierge, fireplaces, hair dryers, ironing facilities, voice mail, tv/vcr.

**Nearby:** Ocean one mile, downtown two blocks.

**Price Range:** $225-$395. AAA, AARP and corporate discounts, off season midweek specials.

**Ivanhoe Inn, 1406 Castillo Street, Santa Barbara, 963-8832.** Owner Mary Robinson is an emergency room nurse in her seventies, who runs her Victorian inn with a little help from her granddaughter and the neighbors. She created a slightly different concept than most B&B's, in that there are no common sitting or eating rooms, so breakfast breads and fruits are delivered to your room. If you want your accommodations to be like new, the Ivanhoe should not be your choice, as Mary does not have time to do the indicated building upkeep. The bathrooms are not luxurious, and the garden could use more attention, but the Ivanhoe has some unique features that attract a steady repeat clientele.

Some of Mary's units are suites, with a smaller second room to accommodate a child or other third person, and she also allows pets. The "Captain's Quarters" has a large living room with a fireplace, an unusual round alcove at one end and a sleeping porch at the other, along with a big master bedroom and full kitchen. Her separate cottage has two bedrooms, living room and full kitchen, small bath and front porch. All units have at least a toaster oven or microwave, coffee maker and small refrigerator, and a welcome bottle of wine is in the fridge. Because of the cooking facilities, the Ivanhoe appeals to people who are in Santa Barbara for several days, as long as they don't expect the building to be immaculately maintained.

**Rooms with Private Bath:** 3.

**Rooms with Shared Bath:** 2.

**Amenities Available:** 2 fireplaces in Captain's Quarters. Limited or full food preparation facilities in all units. Phone available but not in each room. Small tv's in all units except the studio. Free bicycle use.

**Nearby:** Downtown 4 blocks.

**Price Range:** $95-$195. Weekly, monthly, and corporate rates available.

**Old Yacht Club Inn, 431 Corona Del Mar, Santa Barbara, 962-1277, 1-800-549-1676 in Ca., 1-800-676-1676 in the U.S.** This 1912 California craftsman home actually did house the Santa Barbara Yacht Club for awhile, but now a visit there feels more like going to Grandma's house. Opened by four energetic ex-school teachers in 1980, this was Santa Barbara's first B&B. They furnished it with their own family heirlooms and photos, rather than with Laura Ashley. Pink and red predominate, and the effect is a little fussy, but comfortable.

*Beach nuts will love the location of the Old Yacht Club Inn.*

Current owners Eileen and Vince continue the inn's friendly traditions. Many of their customers return again and again, and part of what draws them is the food, and the nightly wine social. Eileen serves the guests a cooked breakfast, and about once a month there is a five-course gourmet Saturday night dinner at an extra charge. The meal is great fun, and some return guests even plan their visit to coincide with a dinner.

**Rooms with Private Baths:** 12.

**Amenities Available:** Private decks, whirlpool tubs. Phones in all rooms. Beach towels and chairs, and bicycles to borrow.

**Nearby:** East Beach one block, Zoo 3 blocks, downtown 1.5 miles.

**Price Range:** $110-$220.

*Some of the rooms at the Parsonage have an ocean view.*

**The Parsonage, 1600 Olive Street, Santa Barbara, 962-9336.** Built in 1892 as a parsonage for Trinity Episcopal Church, this Queen Anne Victorian is now operated as a B & B by Kelly Ebert. She has furnished the public rooms with lovely oriental rugs and fine Victorian antiques. Each bedroom is very different, but all are lovely. The rooms on the second floor are more desirable, as opposed to the two off the main foyer, simply for added privacy. The piece de resistance here is the Honeymoon Suite, which has a luxurious bath and an attached solarium porch, with sweeping views of Santa Barbara looking towards the ocean.

The Parsonage has a covered front porch with wicker seating, and a back deck, where guests can eat their full cooked breakfast or gourmet afternoon hors d'oeuvres.

**Rooms with Private Bath:** 5.

**Amenities Available:** 2 gas stoves, 2 jacuzzi tubs, phone in all rooms.

**Nearby:** Mission 5 blocks, Downtown 8 blocks, beach less than two miles away.

**Price Range:** $85-$295.

**Secret Garden Inn and Cottages, 1908 Bath Street, Santa Barbara, 687-2300, reservations 1-800-676-1622.** The Secret Garden Inn's main building is a large California Craftsman bungalow, where its two least expensive rooms are situated, but most of the accommodations are in the side and back cottages, surrounding a charming garden of winding red brick walkways, ferns and flowers. Frenchwoman Dominique Hannaux purchased the Secret Garden in 1999. She updated the decor with original family paintings, and she occasionally holds art openings at the inn for local artists.

Dominique was raised in a large household in the French Alps by her grandmother, and she uses her grandmother's recipes when making the full cooked buffet breakfast, which is served from 8:30 to 10 a.m. You can eat in the garden, or take it to your room. Like most inns, there's wine and hors d'oeuvres in the afternoon, and they also serve evening cookies or brownies. Like many Santa Barbara B&B's surroundings, the immediate neighborhood is not that scenic, and at the Secret Garden you'll be a few blocks farther from downtown and the beach than at some some other inns. However, if you've come to town to be near Cottage Hospital or Sansum Clinic, this is your most convenient B&B. With a car, what's a few blocks, anyway?

**Rooms with Private Bath:** 11, and a two bedroom vacation rental house by the week or month.

*Only the guests know how nice the Secret Garden really is.*

**Amenities Available:** Fireplaces, porches, private outdoor jacuzzi tubs, television in some rooms. No room phones available.

**Nearby:** Approximately a mile to downtown, same to the Mission.

**Price Range:** $121-$231, weekday discount applies off-season, when their terrific "Getaway" package is also available.

**The Simpson House Inn, 121 East Arrellaga Street, Santa Barbara, 963-7067, 1-800-676-1280.** The Simpson House is quite simply the most gracious, tranquil and enchanting of the Santa Barbara inns. It sits in a nicer neighborhood than most other B&B's, thanks to the owners' persistence in bending the zoning laws. The Simpson House has larger grounds and more privacy than most inns, and it's just a few steps from three square blocks of beautiful parks.

The Simpson House has grown to fourteen rooms in the last few years, so it now has the feel of a boutique luxury inn, rather than a traditional B&B. In addition to the original 1874 Eastlake Victorian, which is opulently furnished and bedecked with covered porches, the most luxurious accommodations are now located in the reconstructed barn and the new cottages at the back of the property. The barn rooms are extremely spacious, while the cottages are cozier, and are the priciest because of their jacuzzi tubs and rock fireplaces. The owners, Glyn and Linda Davies, designed most of the new rooms themselves, and they stopped just short of being "cutesy." Everything is exquisitely charming.

The garden is wonderful, with multiple sitting areas, winding paths, and fountains. The staff is genteel and friendly, and the breakfast is good and can be taken in the garden, dining room or in your room. They serve wine and hors d'oeuvres every day, and not just cheese and crackers. They may have up to fifteen items to sample, but be sure to save room so you can try one of Santa Barbara's great restaurants for dinner.

**Rooms with Private Baths:** 15. One room has a detached bath.

**Amenities Available:** Private balconies, jacuzzi tubs, fireplaces, TV/VCR's. Phones in all rooms, refrigerators, hair dryers, robes.

**Nearby:** Parks half block, downtown 4 blocks, beach 15 blocks.

**Price Range:** $215-$550.

**Tiffany Inn, 1323 De La Vina Street, Santa Barbara, 963-2283, 1-800-999-5672.** The Tiffany Inn is a stately old home with Victorian and Craftsman touches, conveniently located near downtown, the Art Museum and the Courthouse. It has a lovely tree-shaded deck in the garden, where a full breakfast is usually served from 8 to 10 a.m. The proprietors offer wine and cheese before dinner time, and cookies when you return in the evening.

The home's living and dining rooms are gracious, and all of the guest rooms are pleasant. In fact, the entire inn is maintained to a very good standard. Perhaps the Master Suite is most interesting, as it is located in the converted attic. It has coved ceilings, a private third floor deck, fireplace, television, and a jacuzzi tub. Those who are romantically inclined should note that the Honeymoon Suite isn't really a suite at all. It's a rather dark but sweet room with a fireplace, a jacuzzi tub for two, and a small private porch. Even cocooning honeymooners will probably appreciate the Tiffany's location, just a stroll from all of Santa Barbara's downtown charms.

**Rooms with Private Bath:** 7.

**Amenities Available:** Fireplaces, jacuzzi tubs, balconies or porches, televisions. Clock radios and phones in all rooms.

**Nearby:** Downtown 2 blocks.

**Price Range:** $145-$325. Corporate rates available.

**The Upham, 1404 De La Vina Street, Santa Barbara, 962-0058.** With 50 rooms, you might think it's a stretch to call the Upham a B&B. But since this is the oldest continuously operating hotel in Santa Barbara, harking back to 1871, the overriding feeling is one of well-tended quaintness. In fact, back when Abraham Lincoln's cousin owned it, the Chinese cook would stand up top in the widow's walk with a telescope, watching Stearns Wharf to see how many guests were arriving by ship for dinner!

The cozy lobby is done in shades of colonial gray, and rooms are decorated nicely with plantation shutters and antiques. They're sprinkled around in several buildings, with some rooms being quieter than others, so ask if you're sensitive to street noise.

One of the Upham's drawing cards is its courtyard garden with

*The Upham, in business since 1871, is the oldest continuously operating hotel in Santa Barbara.*

chairs for lolling about. Breakfast is of the expanded continental variety and is available until late morning. It may be eaten in the lobby, on the porch, in the garden or your room. They serve wine and cheese for cocktail hour, and oreo cookies and milk for those with later-night munchies. Another plus is the presence of Louie's, an excellent restaurant serving dinner daily, just in case you're in the mood to laze around and never leave the hotel.

**Rooms with Private Bath:** 50.

**Amenities Available:** Fireplaces, jacuzzi tubs, balconies or porches. Television, phone, and clock radio in all rooms.

**Nearby:** Downtown 2 blocks.

**Price Range:** $150-$400 on week-ends. 25% weekday discount, subject to availability. 10% AAA discount.

**Villa Rosa, 15 Chapala Street, Santa Barbara, 966-0851.** The Villa Rosa has the feel of a small hotel, but offers many of the features of a bed and breakfast. Situated half a block from the ocean, near Stearns Wharf and the harbor, this remodelled Spanish-style apartment building offers more privacy than most B&B's, along with a lovely courtyard pool and spa.

The interior is done in sandy, subdued colors with an understated southwest motif. In some areas, notably the entrance hall, it could use a coat of paint, but the rooms are comfortable and attractive, and have some fun features. There's even a two story suite that sleeps four, and has a living room and kitchenette.

Continental breakfast is served from 7 to 10 a.m. in the lounge, or you can have it brought to your room. There's wine and cheese from 5 to 7 p.m., and port and sherry later in the evening. Villa Rosa is recommended for those who want to experience a hostelry other than a large hotel, and prefer modern accommodations. If you want a beach area room, the Villa Rosa is very well located.

**Rooms with Private Bath:** 18.

**Amenities Available:** Fireplaces, kitchenette, balconies. Phones, newspapers, hairdryers and robes in all rooms. Kids 14 and up allowed.

**Nearby:** half block to ocean, 6 blocks to downtown, 2 blocks to Amtrak station.

**Price Range:** $125-$260.

*Those who want Spanish charm mixed with modern conveniences will enjoy Villa Rosa.*

**Inn on Summer Hill, 2520 Lillie Avenue, Summerland, 969-9998, 1-800-845-5566.** Here is the place for those who want an extremely cozy and attractive escape, and don't care about being right in Santa Barbara. In fact, the Inn on Summer Hill in Summerland (see "Metamorphosis: Spooksville to Antique Alley" on page ?) is one of the more luxurious small inns in the area. Unlike most B&B's in Santa Barbara, the New England-style building was constructed in the modern era to be an inn, so all the comforts are present.

Mabel Shults and her husband Paul are the owners, and Mabel is quite a well-known, prominent interior designer, having specialized in hotel design for years. It shows. The decor is eye-catching, intricate and tasteful. Every room has a canopy bed, fireplace, T.V. with V.C.R., air conditioning, whirlpool tub, phone, stereo cassette player, refrigerator, bathrobes, ironing boards, hairdryers, and boiling water faucets! There's an ocean view, and the soundproofing effectively blocks out the freeway noise, unless you're on your balcony or in the jacuzzi. First floor rooms are more cozy because they have lower pine ceilings, while the upstairs rooms have cathedral pine ceilings, and therefore a more airy look.

*The Inn on Summer Hill's decor is comfortably opulent.*

Breakfast is served from 7 a.m. to 10 a.m. in the dining room, or for a $5 per person charge you may have it in your room. Don't miss the amazing teapot collection. There's wine and cheese from 3 to 5 p.m., and you may wish to use their outdoor jacuzzi before picking out a movie to watch from their video library. Although this inn is a little off the beaten track, you'll love it if you're more interested in relaxing than seeing the sights of Santa Barbara, and you don't want to put up with any of the creaky idiosyncracies of older B&B houses.

**Rooms with Private Bath:** 16.

**Amenities Available:** See above.

**Nearby:** Antique stores, Summerland Beach, Santa Barbara Polo & Racquet Club (polo match info 684-8667). Santa Barbara is ten minutes away.

**Price Range:** $229-339. AAA, corporate and senior discounts available weekdays.

**Summerland Inn, 2161 Ortega Hill Road, Summerland, 969-5225.** The Summerland Inn has a less than scenic location, sandwiched next to a retail/office building and the freeway. Another inn that was built a few years back as a B&B, it lacks the creakiness of some Victorian B&B's. Some will miss that wonderful antique quality, while others don't want to put up with building eccentricities. Guests here have the run of the living room, dining room, and even the kitchen is available for its fridge and microwave. A continental breakfast is served between 8:30 and 10:30 a.m., with cookies on offer in the afternoon.

Rooms are comfortable and nicely furnished. Be sure to book one of the rooms away from the freeway to escape the car noise, as their soundproofing is not state of the art. At least the beach, restaurants and antique shops are within walking distance.

**Rooms with Private Bath:** 13.

Amenities Available: Fireplaces. Television and phone in all rooms.

**Nearby:** See Inn on Summer Hill.

**Price Range:** $65-205. 10% AAA, corporate and AARP discounts.

**Prufrock's Garden Inn, 600 Linden Avenue, Carpinteria, 566-9696.** Jim and Judy Halvorsen used to work at Westmont College in Montecito, but in 1995 Judy left the academic arena to open this bright, cheery B&B in a 1904 Craftsman bungalow near the beach. Later, Jim followed her, to devote more time to their inn. It's clear that they spend a lot of time keeping the house and gardens in pristine shape. That's not surprising, since before opening they spent every waking moment for four months preparing the house, including a week and a half doing nothing but refinishing door hardware. The decor is beachy yet tasteful, and the garden offers comfortable seating. There are also two cottage rooms, that offer patio fireplaces and jacuzzi tubs.

Rates include a full cooked breakfast, as well as hors d'oeuvres and nonalcoholic beverages later in the day, and 24 hour sweet treats are available.

Directions: Exit 101 at Linden Avenue, and head towards the ocean. Prufrock's is at the corner of Linden and 6th Street.

**Rooms with Private Baths:** 5.

**Rooms with Shared Baths:** 2.

**Amenities Available:** Robes, hair dryers, irons, fresh flowers. Prufrock's stresses the simple life, but some rooms have TV's, and phones are available upon request.

**Nearby:** Downtown Carpinteria shops and restaurants, two blocks to Carpinteria Beach, near Amtrak, fifteen minutes drive to Santa Barbara.

**Price Range:** $89-$299, ask about specials and packages.

**Ballard Inn, 2436 Baseline Avenue, Ballard, 688-7770, 800-638-2466.** Newly built as an inn in 1984, this is one of the few bed and breakfasts that also offers dinner Wednesday through Sunday in its Cafe Chardonnay. For those staying more than one night, the Ballard Inn is close to excellent restaurants in Santa Ynez, and to the Vintage Room in Los Olivos.

Each room here has a different theme, such as the Vineyard Room or the Western Room, but the designer stopped short of a Disneyland effect. All rooms are attractive and very spacious, and are furnished with antiques.

*The Ballard Inn tempts its guests with afternoon wine and hors d'oeuvres.*

The tiny hamlet of Ballard is an excellent location from which to explore the wineries, and to bicycle around the valley (bring your own). Prospective guests should note that other than dining, there is nothing much to do in the area in the evening, unless the Solvang Theaterfest is in session. If you want to stroll around after dinner and window shop or people watch, see a play or concert or go dancing, a Santa Barbara inn might suit you better. But if you're looking for a secluded, romantic getaway, this could be just right.

**Rooms with Private Bath:** 15.

**Amenities Available:** Fireplaces. Televisions and phones upon request. Hair dryers and irons in all rooms.

**Nearby:** Wineries, Los Olivos art galleries, Solvang and other valley attractions are minutes away by car.

**Price Range:** $195-275.

**Fess Parker's Wine Country Inn & Spa, 2860 Grand Ave., Los Olivos, 688-7788, 1-800-446-2455.** This deluxe inn opened in 1985 as the Los Olivos Grand Hotel, and quickly made Los Olivos a choice week-end destination for art lovers wishing to visit the town's collection of galleries. It is also perfectly situated for bicycle riding, and touring the valley's many wineries.

All rooms are quite large and have a fireplace. In 2002, owners Fess and Marcie Parker redecorated in sophisticated French Country, and they've added a gift shop, and a spa in a cottage down the street. Yes, this is the Fess you will remember from television shows about Davey Crockett and Dan'l Boone. For years now, Fess has been a successful real estate developer in the area. He built and retains a large interest in Santa Barbara's Doubletree Resort, and he also created a large winery on his ranch, not far from the Wine Country Inn.

An expanded continental breakfast is included in the room rates. Also, the inn has an excellent restaurant, The Vintage Room, which serves all three meals.

**Rooms with Private Bath:** 21.

**Amenities Available:** Spa tubs. Public facilities include pool and outdoor jacuzzi, and dining room with verandah. Television, phone, a bottle of Fess Parker's wine, and fireplaces in all rooms, plus free wine tasting for two at his winery. Nearby: Art galleries, historic Mattei's Tavern, wineries, Solvang (ten minutes away).

**Price Range:** $250-450.

**Theodore Woolsey House, 1484 E. Ojai Avenue, Ojai, 646-9779.** A former professor and dean of Yale University, Theodore Woolsey built his huge old farmhouse in 1887, after moving to Ojai in hopes of improving his wife's poor health. It didn't work in her case, but Ojai is still known as a place to "destress."

Since 1987, Ana Cross has worked to restore Woolsey's home while keeping its countrified character. It has a comfortable living room and large dining room, where an expanded continental breakfast is served from 8:30 to 10:30. There are also charming screened porches in back which overlook the pool. Ana has installed a putting green, horseshoe pit, volleyball court, and croquet area, as well as an outdoor jacuzzi, so there are plenty of amusements. The property's seven acres also include hundred year old oak trees, and a nice garden.

Woolsey House is not a slick, frilly Victorian-style inn. The fir floors creak, the neighbor's rooster crows sometimes, and some

*Theodore Woolsey House offers a real country house experience, with a pool and jacuzzi on the side.*

"private" bathrooms are not connected to the rooms. If you are concerned about privacy, ask for an exact description of the layout. One room, for example, has a detached bathroom, but it is in a totally private area of the house, right next to the upstairs deck. A lot of people find this old time country house experience to be a fun one, because week-ends book up several weeks ahead of time.

**Rooms with Private Bath:** 6, some with detached baths, and a cottage room.

**Amenities Available:** Fireplaces, private balconies. Television and phone in 4 rooms. Central air conditioning.

**Nearby:** Two golf courses, downtown Ojai, Libbey Park.

**Price Range:** $65-175.

**Bella Maggiore Inn, 67 South California Street, Ventura, 652-0277, 1-800-523-8479 for reservations.** This small historic hotel in the heart of downtown Ventura does not have the typical frilly B & B look. In fact, its architect also designed the former Grauman's Chinese Theatre, and the venerable Ventura

City Hall. The building was beautifully renovated in 1984, and the only feature they were unable to completely update is the very slight musty smell that often is in older structures. Room decor is understated but comfortable, and rates include a full breakfast cooked to order in their attractive restaurant, Nona's Courtyard Cafe. Those who love antique shopping, or who wish to attend a concert at the Ventura Theatre and not drive afterwards, will love this location.

**Rooms with Private Bath:** 28.

**Amenities Available:** Fireplaces, jacuzzi tubs, wet bars, microwaves, refrigerators. Television and phone in all rooms.

**Nearby:** Beach 3 blocks, downtown surrounds the inn.

**Price Range:** $75-175. AAA, senior and corporate discounts.

# Visitor Centers

**Lompoc Valley Chamber of Commerce**
111 South "I" Street
736-4567
www.lompoc.com
9 a.m. to 5 p.m., Monday through Friday.

**Ojai Valley Chamber of Commerce and Visitors Center**
150 West Ojai Avenue
646-8126
www.the-ojai.org
9:30 a.m. to 4:30 p.m. Monday to Friday, 10 a.m. to 4 p.m. Saturday and Sunday.

**Oxnard Convention & Visitors Bureau**
200 West 7th Street
385-7545 or 1-800-2OXNARD
www.oxnardtourism.com
8:30 a.m. to 5 p.m., Monday through Friday, closed 12-1 p.m

**Oxnard Factory Outlet Visitor Center**
Friday through Sunday, 11 a.m.-4 p.m.

**Santa Barbara Chamber of Commerce Visitor Center**
1 Garden Street
965-3021
www.santabarbaraca.com
9 a.m. to 5 p.m. (4 p.m. during the holidays, 6 p.m. in summer) Monday to Saturday, 10 a.m. to 5 p.m. Sunday.

**Santa Paula Chamber of Commerce**
200 N. Tenth St.
525-5561
www.santapaulachamber.com
9 a.m. to 5 p.m. weekdays, 11 a.m. to 4 p.m. weekends.

**Solvang Conference & Visitors Bureau**
1511A Mission Drive
688-6144, 1-800-468-6765
www.solvangusa.com
10 a.m. to 4 p.m. daily.

**Ventura Visitors & Convention Bureau**
89-C S. California Street
648-2075 or 1-800-333-2989
www.ventura-usa.com
8:30 a.m. to 5 p.m. Monday through Friday, 9 a.m. to 5 p.m. Saturday, 10 - 4 Sunday.

# Geographical Index

**Santa Maria**



**Santa Paula**

# Alphabetical Index